MOSAIC Crochet

MODERN BLANKETS IN OVERLAY MOSAIC

ANA MORAIS SOARES

Tuva Publishing

www.tuvapublishing.com

Address Merkez Mah. Cavusbasi Cad. No 71
Cekmekoy - Istanbul 34782 / Turkey
Tel +9 0216 642 62 62

Mosaic Crochet

First Print 2023 / August

All Global Copyrights Belong To
Tuva Tekstil ve Yayıncılık Ltd.

Content Crochet

Editor in Chief Ayhan DEMİRPEHLİVAN

Project Editor Kader DEMİRPEHLİVAN

Designer Ana Morais Soares

Technical Editor Leyla ARAS

Graphic Designers Ömer ALP, Abdullah BAYRAKÇI,
Tarık TOKGÖZ, Yunus GÜLDOĞAN

Photography Tuva Publishing

Crochet Tech Editor Wendi CUSINS

Photo Styling Çiğdem TALİPOĞLU

ISBN 978-605-7834-68-3

 TuvaYayincilik    TuvaPublishing

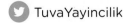 TuvaYayincilik    TuvaPublishing

THANK YOU

Besides my family, who always support me in my designing adventures, I want to thank my lovely testing team. These ladies worked so hard testing and making all the blankets from the book. More than testers, they are friends. Thank you, **Edith Horn** (who also helped me with pattern edits), **Heather Vold**, **Joanne Borden**, **Jodi Ross**, and **Sally Murray**. You are all amazing! Also, a big thank you to **Wendi Cusins** for her amazing edit work.

DEDICATION

This book is dedicated to my lovely and gentle mother who still has fun watching my designs grow and keeps having patience to deal with all my doubts. Love you, Mom. ♥

CONTENTS

MOSAIC CROCHET

GENERAL PATTERN NOTES

STARTING YOUR PROJECT

PROJECTS

INTRODUCTION

I have been a crafty woman, ever since I can remember. I love everything about yarn, hooks, needles, and fabrics. And this crafting passion started very early, with two women to blame - my grandmother and my mother.

As a child, I remember those early afternoons at my grandmother's house, with my mother, her sisters, and my great-aunts all sitting together, chatting and crocheting. You may not believe it, but these women always had something on their hooks! We would take a break in the middle of the daily crocheting session to have a snack with coffee, juice, hot bread, and cake. Sweet moments in all aspects.

Crafting can be so therapeutic that nowadays many doctors recommend it to their patients. It helps to reduce the daily stress and keeps our minds occupied.

And what to say about color?!!! Have you ever noticed how you choose one color palette instead of another? In my case, I go for a pastel palette when I am feeling more sentimental; and when I am feeling full of energy, I choose a bright palette. Colors work magic and can help us restore our mood.

So, why not use colors in crochet for healing?!!! This is where Mosaic Crochet can do wonders. You can mix all different colors that will never be wrong with each other. The more contrast the better.

I present to you my second crochet book. It is all about my addiction to Mosaic Crochet. I hope you love the blanket patterns created for the book and that you have lots of fun making them.

Sending love

PROJECT GALLERY

Fluffy Snowflakes P.26

Chocolate Gems P.34

Tiles P.42

Tutti Frutti P.50

Between Waves P.58

Rolling Diamonds P.66

Winter Elements P.74

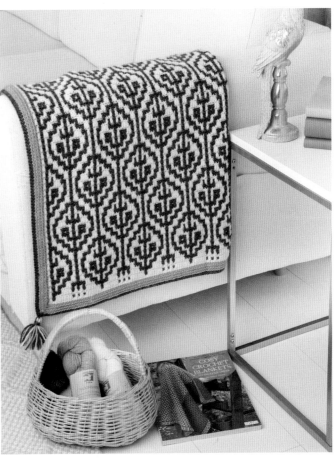

In My Garden P.88

9

MOSAIC CROCHET

Easy, fun, modern and elegant, is how I describe Mosaic Crochet. You may have seen the two mosaic patterns in my previous book, "Cosy Crochet Blankets to Snuggle Under", released in 2019. I really enjoyed designing and making those blankets and since then, Mosaic Crochet has become my go-to technique of choice. Not only is it addictive, it is also relaxing to do. Almost anybody can master this technique, it is so easy to learn. But be aware... Once you try it, you probably won't be able to stop!

Mosaic Crochet is a colorful crochet technique. It entails working rows (or rounds) using different colors to create the lovely patterns. For a visual impact, a minimum of two colors is required. The more contrasting the colors are, the better. This technique differs from Tapestry Crochet, another colorful crochet technique, which carries the unused colors across the rows or rounds until needed. In Mosaic Crochet, there is no switching of colors in mid-row (or round).

Although it looks difficult to do, Mosaic Crochet is in fact very easy. With only two basic crochet stitches - single crochet stitch and double crochet stitch – you can create beautiful blankets. If this is your first attempt at Mosaic Crochet, do not worry, as this book has step-by-step tutorials – with photographs – making it easy for you to learn the technique. Each of the blanket patterns include both the written instructions, as well as the accompanying stitch chart for you to follow.

There are two common types of Mosaic Crochet – Inset Mosaic and Overlay Mosaic.

Inset Mosaic Crochet uses two rows in each color. The first row comprises of single crochet stitches and chain stitches, with double crochet stitches worked in front of the chain spaces into the skipped single crochet stitches three rows below. The second row uses only single crochet and chain stitches.

Overlay Mosaic Crochet is worked with the right side always facing you and only one row or round is worked for each color. The blankets in this book are made using the Overlay Mosaic technique.

Overlay Mosaic Crochet

A basic description of the technique is that short stitches (usually single crochet stitches) are worked in the back loops of the stitches on the previous row, leaving the front loops available. Long stitches (usually double crochet stitches) are then worked "over" the short stitches into the available front loops, generally two rows below. The long stitches "lie over" the short stitches, hence the word "overlay crochet".

■ When working Overlay Mosaic in rows, the yarn is cut at the end of each row, and the piece is never turned. The next row starts by joining the yarn in the first stitch made on the previous row. There are yarn tails at the beginning and end of each row, creating a "fringe" on both sides of the piece. This fringe can be trimmed as a decorative edging, or, more commonly, a double border is worked around the blanket to "hide" the tails.

General Notes for Overlay Mosaic Crochet

■   The technique can be worked in either rows or rounds.

■   The rows or rounds are ALWAYS worked with the right side facing you. *Do not turn your work at the end of the row or round.*

■   Each row or round is worked in one color only. Generally, each row or round alternates between two contrasting colors.

■   Single crochet stitches are worked in the back loop only (except for the Border Stitches). The double crochet stitches are worked in the front loop only of the corresponding stitch two rows below. Stitches behind the double crochet stitches are always skipped.

■   When working in rows, the yarn is joined to the piece with a standing single crochet stitch at the beginning of the row, leaving a tail. At the end of each row, the yarn is cut and secured with a chain stitch, leaving another tail. The tails must be at least two inches (five centimeters) long.

■   When working in rounds (making Motifs), the unused yarn color is carried up at the back of the piece.

■   A Double Border (also known as an Enclosed Border or Envelope Border) can be added to a piece which has been worked in rows to hide the tails. The border is worked in rounds.

STICHES & TERMINOLOGY USED IN MOSAIC CROCHET

This book uses US Crochet Terminology

US vs UK terminology:

US	UK
Chain Stitch (ch)	Chain Stitch (ch)
Slip Stitch (sl st)	Slip Stitch (sl st)
Single crochet (sc)	Double crochet (dc)
Half-double crochet (hdc)	Half-treble (htr)
Double Crochet (dc)	Treble (tr)

Symbols Used	Definition
Repeat from * to **	The instruction/s between * and ** are repeated the number of times specified.
[...]	Square brackets indicate the main repeat across the row. Repeat the instructions inside the brackets the required number of times.
(...)	Round brackets mark a small repeat within the main repeat. Repeat the instructions inside the brackets as many times as indicated.

Abbreviation	Basic Stitches
ch / chs	Chain stitch(es)
sl st	Slip stitch
sc	Single Crochet
hdc	Half-Double Crochet
dc	Double Crochet

Abbreviation	Term
Rnd	Round
sp / sps	Space(s)
st / sts	Stitch(es)
"	Inch(es)

Special Stitches	
Back Loop Only (BLO)	Insert the hook from front to back under only the loop furthest from you.
Front Loop Only (FLO)	Insert the hook from front to back under only the loop nearest to you.
Border Stitch (BS)	Work the first and last stitch of a row through both loops of the stitch on the previous row.

Standing Stitches	
Standing Slip Stitch	Start with a slip knot on the hook. Insert the hook in the stitch or space specified and pull the yarn through the stitch or space, drawing the yarn through the loop on the hook, to complete the slip stitch.
Standing Single Crochet	Start with a slip knot on the hook. Insert the hook in the stitch or space specified and pull up a loop (two loops on the hook). Yarn over and draw through both loops on the hook to complete the single crochet stitch.
Standing Double Crochet	Start with a slip knot on the hook. Yarn over, insert the hook in the stitch or space specified and pull up a loop (three loops on the hook). Yarn over hook and draw through two loops on the hook (two loops on hook). Yarn over hook and draw through remaining two loops to complete the double crochet stitch.

OVERLAY MOSAIC CROCHET STITCH CHARTS

Most patterns for Overlay designs come with a stitch chart. This is a visual representation of the design. At first glance it might seem daunting, but they are fairly easy to read and follow.

It is advantageous to know how to read both charts and written patterns. If the pattern doesn't make sense, check it against the stitch chart (or vice versa).

Pratice Swatch

BS	5	4	3	2	1	E	E	BS	Color	Row
			x	x					C1	R9
	x		x			x			C2	R8
		x				x	x		C1	R7
			x						C2	R6
	x		x			x			C1	R5
	x			x			x		C2	R4
			x	x					C1	R3
									C2	R2
									C1	FR/R1
BS	5	4	3	2	1	E	E	BS		

Repeat

Legend:
- ☐ sc in BLO
- ▨ Border Stitch (BS)
- ⊠ dc in FLO, 2 rows down
- E Extra Stitch
- ▨ C2

How to Interpret a Stitch Chart

A stitch chart contains all the information you need to make a project. Within a chart, each block represents one worked stitch, and a row of blocks represents one row of the written pattern.

Looking at the chart and legend:

- To the right of the chart, the Row numbers and Colors used are shown.

- Two colors of yarn are identified – Color 1 (White) and Color 2 (Green).

- Along the bottom of the chart, the two blocks with "BS" indicate the position of the Border Stitches in the chart – the first and last stitch of each row. These stitches are worked through both loops of the stitch below. After the first Border Stitch is a Chain Stitch, and before the last Border Stitch is another Chain Stitch. Within the chart, the Border Stitches and Chains are shown as a pink block.

- Along the bottom of the chart, the blocks with "E" indicate the position of the "Extra" stitches (those outside of the stitch repeat pattern) within the chart.

- The yellow highlighted blocks indicate the position of the repeated pattern stitches within each chart row.

- In the chart, blocks with an "X" (which can be in either color) indicate a double crochet stitch worked in the front loop only, two rows down.

- The "open" blocks in the chart (which can be in either color), are those blocks which have no letter or symbol in them. These blocks indicate a single crochet stitch worked in the back loop only.

How to Follow a Stitch Chart

Note: Use the chart labelled "Practice Chart". The written pattern associated with this chart is under Starting Your Project – A Practice Swatch – complete with photo tutorials.

A chart is read from the bottom to the top and also from the right to the left. Each chart row is worked in one color only – as identified next to the Row Number. For example, the entire Row 2 (R2) is worked in Color 2 (C2).

Looking at the chart, starting at the bottom row and reading from right to left:

The Foundation Row / Row 1, use Color 1 and needs the required number of foundation stitches – either using Foundation Single Crochet or working single crochet stitches in a chain string.

Row 2 uses Color 2 and starts with a pink block – a Border Stitch, which is a single crochet worked through both loops, followed by a chain stitch.

Across the row are open blocks - single crochet stitches worked in the back loop only. (Even though some open blocks are "white", only Color 2 is used for the whole row.)

The last block is pink, which is another Border Stitch – a single crochet worked through both loops (after working a chain stitch).

Row 3 (uses Color 1 across the row) starts with a Border Stitch, and two (Extra) stitches – both single crochet (worked in back loop only). The five-stitch repeat pattern is:
   One single crochet stitch (worked in the back loop only).
   Two double crochet stitches (worked in front loop only of the corresponding stitches on Row 1).
   Two single crochet stitches (worked in the back loop only).
   Repeat these five stitches until the last stitch. The last stitch is a Border Stitch (after working a chain stitch).

Row 4 (uses Color 2) and after the Border Stitch (and chain stitch), the Extra Stitches are a double crochet (in the front loop only of the corresponding stitch on Row 2) and a single crochet (back loop only). The five stitch repeat is:
   Double crochet (FLO on Row 2)
   Two single crochets (BLO)
   Double crochet (FLO on Row 2)
   Single crochet (BLO)

After the final repeat, work the last Border Stitch (after working a chain stitch).

Row 5: (uses Color 1)
   Border Stitch (and ch-1), sc (BLO), dc (FLO on Row 3),
   Repeat sts: 2 sc (BLO), dc (FLO Row 3), sc (BLO),
   dc (FLO Row 3)

After all the repeats are done, make a chain stitch and work a Border Stitch in the last stitch.

Row 6: (Color 2) Border Stitch (and ch-1), 2 sc (BLO),
   Repeat sts: sc (BLO), dc (FLO Row 4), 3 sc (BLO)
   After repeats, ch 1 & Border Stitch.

We know that all single crochets are worked in BLO and double crochets in FLO two rows down... And we know that the Border Stitches include a chain stitch... So, things start looking like the written pattern.

Row 7: (C1) BS & ch 1, dc, sc,
   Repeat sts: dc, 2 sc, dc, sc
   After repeats, ch 1 & BS.

The repeated stitches are now placed in square brackets...

Row 8: (C2) BS & ch 1, 1 sc, 1 dc, [2 sc, 1 dc, 1 sc, 1 dc] x times, ch 1 & BS.

Row 9: (C1) BS & ch 1, 2 sc, [2 dc, 3 sc] x times times, ch 1 & BS.

GENERAL PATTERN NOTES

- All the blankets which are worked in rows, are designed with a "**repeat pattern**" across the rows. At the beginning and end of the rows can be some extra stitches (excluding the Border Stitches) which help create a symmetric layout.

- The instructions for the repeat pattern are between square brackets and the stitches highlighted.

- The **Border Stitches (BS)** are worked through both loops of the stitches.

- One **chain stitch** is made after the beginning Border Stitch and another **chain stitch** before the last Border Stitch. (*Hint: Use a stitch marker on each chain to remind you to work the chain stitches.*)
These chain stitches are NOT included in the stitch counts for the rows.

- All **single crochet stitches** (except the two Border Stitches) are worked through the **back loop** only.

- All **double crochet stitches** (except on the back layer of the border rounds) are worked through the **front loop** of the corresponding stitch two rows below. (*For example, the double crochet stitches of Row 5 are worked in the front loop only of the stitches on Row 3.*)

- The stitches **behind** the double crochet stitches of the row are always **skipped**.

- When working the border, the slip stitches of the **Special Round** are worked in the **chain spaces** created after the first Border Stitch and before the last Border Stitch.

TIPS & TECHNIQUES

Foundation Single Crochet (FSC)

Foundation stitches are also known as the "chainless foundation". Usually the first row of crochet stitches are worked into a chain foundation. Here the chain stitch and the crochet stitch of the first row are worked simultaneously.

Advantages of using the Foundation Single Crochet Method

a) It creates a flexible and stretchy foundation row with better tension than when the first row of stitches is worked into a string of chain stitches.

b) As the foundation stitches are more "elastic", your foundation row will have the same length as the other rows.

c) There is no need to worry about having too many or too few chain stitches, as you can easily add extra FSC stitches or frog (pull out) stitches at the end of the foundation row when working the second row.

Note: Do not cut the yarn after the foundation row, until you have completed the second row and checked your stitch count.

d) The Foundation Single Crochet method gives your project a more beautiful and professional look.

How to work Foundation Single Crochet

1. With a slip knot on the hook, make two chain stitches.

2. Insert the hook into the first chain stitch (under two loops – the top loop and back bump of the chain stitch) and pull up a loop (two loops on the hook). *Image 1*

3. Yarn over hook, and draw yarn through the first loop on the hook (**base chain stitch made**). *Images 2 & 3*

4. Yarn over hook and draw through both loops on hook to complete the single crochet stitch (**first FSC made**). *Images 4 & 5*

5. Insert the hook under the outer two loops (top loop and back bump) of the base chain stitch made and pull up a loop (two loops on hook). *Images 6-8*

6. Yarn over hook, and draw yarn through the first loop on the hook (**next base chain stitch made**). *Image 9*

7. Yarn over hook and draw through both loops on hook to complete single crochet (**next FSC made**).

8. Repeat Steps 5-7 until desired length is reached. *Images 10 & 11*

Double Border

- A Double Border consists of a front layer and a back layer, which are then joined together.

- Before making the border, you need to work a round of slip stitches (Special Round) on the front of the blanket.

- The first round of the front layer is worked with the right side facing and uses single crochet stitches into the furthest loop of the slip stitches of the Special Round.

- The first round of the back layer is worked with the wrong side facing and uses double crochet stitches worked into the "back loops" of the slip stitches made on the Special Round.

- The Joining Round is worked using slip stitches catching the back loops of the corresponding stitches from both layers.

Making the Double Border

1. Secure the Yarn Tails:

a) Tie two yarn tails together using a double knot to secure. Trim the ends to approximately 1" (2 cm) long. *If you prefer you can do this before joining the two layers of the border, but be careful to not cut your work. Image 12*

2. Work the Special Round (slip stitches):

a) With the right side of blanket facing you and using the indicated color in the pattern, start with a standing slip stitch in the first stitch on the Foundation Row/Row 1 (bottom edge). Make two chains and slip stitch in the same stitch. *(First corner made.)* Mark the chain-2 corner space with a stitch marker. *Image 13*

b) Working across the **right edge** of the blanket, work a slip stitch in each chain-space (created after the Border Stitch) across to the last row. *Image 14*

c) On the last row, slip stitch in the chain-space, make two chains and then slip stitch in the back loop only of the chain-stitch itself. *(Second corner made.)* Mark the chain-2 corner space with a stitch marker. *Image 15*

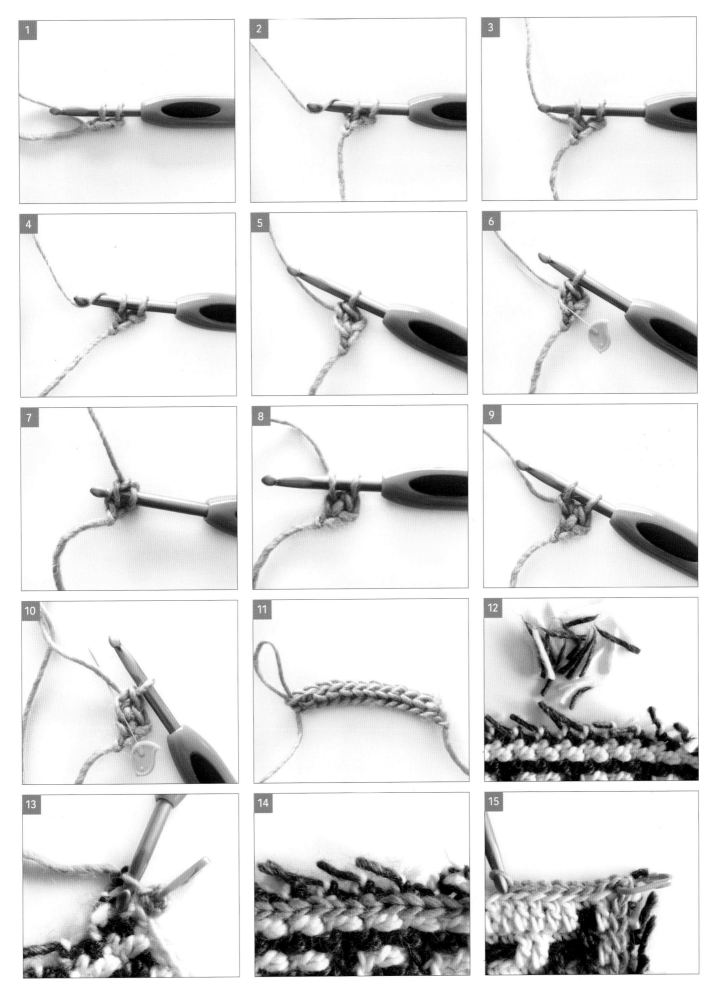

d) Working across the **top edge** of the blanket, slip stitch in the back loop only of each stitch across to the chain-space before the Border Stitch. *Image 15*

e) Slip stitch in the back loop only of the chain stitch, make two chains and slip stitch in the same chain-space. *(Third corner made.)* Mark the chain-2 corner space with a stitch marker. *Image 16*

f) Working across the **left edge**, slip stitch in each chain-space (created before the Border Stitch) across to the Foundation Row/Row 1.

g) Work a slip stitch in last stitch on the Foundation Row/Row 1, make two chains and slip stitch in the same stitch. *(Fourth corner made.)* Mark the chain-2 corner space with a stitch marker. *Images 17 & 18*

h) Working along the **bottom edge**, slip stitch in each stitch across. Join the round with a slip stitch in the first corner chain-2 space. Cut the yarn. *Image 19*

3. Work the Back Layer of the Border:

With the wrong side of the blanket facing you, the first round of double crochet stitches are worked in the loops created by the slip stitches. Image 20

a) Start with a standing double crochet in any corner chain-2 space, created in the Special Round. Work another double crochet in the same space, then make two chains, and work two more double crochets in the same space. *Image 21*

b) Work a double crochet in each loop around, and in each corner chain-2 space, work 2 double crochets, 2 chain stitches & 2 double crochets. *(Take care not to skip the back slip stitches before and after the corner chain-2 spaces.)* At the end of the round, join with a slip stitch to the top of the first double crochet. *Image 22*

c) Following the blanket pattern, work the next rounds (either single or double crochet) through both loops of the stitches.

4. Work the Front Layer of the Border:

With the right side of the blanket facing you, the first round of single crochet stitches are worked in the back loop only of the slip stitches.

The corners are worked in the same chain spaces as the Back Layer double crochet stitches. The first single crochet of the corner is worked in the space before the double crochet stitches, and the second single crochet of the corner is worked in the same space after the double crochet stitches. Image 23

a) In any corner space, start with a standing single crochet in the space before the double crochet stitches, make two chains, and work another single crochet in the same space after the double crochet stitches. *Image 24*

b) Work a single crochet stitch in the back loop only of the slip stitches all around, working (single crochet, chain 2, single crochet) in each corner space *(as described)*. *Images 25 & 26*

c) Following the pattern, the next rounds are worked as follows: All single crochet stitches are worked in the back loop only, except for the corners, which are worked in the corner chain-2 spaces.

If the border has a mosaic pattern, all double crochet stitches are worked in the front loop of the corresponding stitch two rounds below.

5. Join the Front and Back Layers:

The joining round is worked with the right side of the blanket facing you.

a) In any corner space, start with a standing single crochet. *Image 27*

b) Work two more single crochet-stitches in same space. *Image 28*

c) Working through the back loop only of both the front and corresponding back stitch, slip stitch in each stitch around, working 3 single crochet stitches in each corner chain-2 space. *Images 29 & 30*

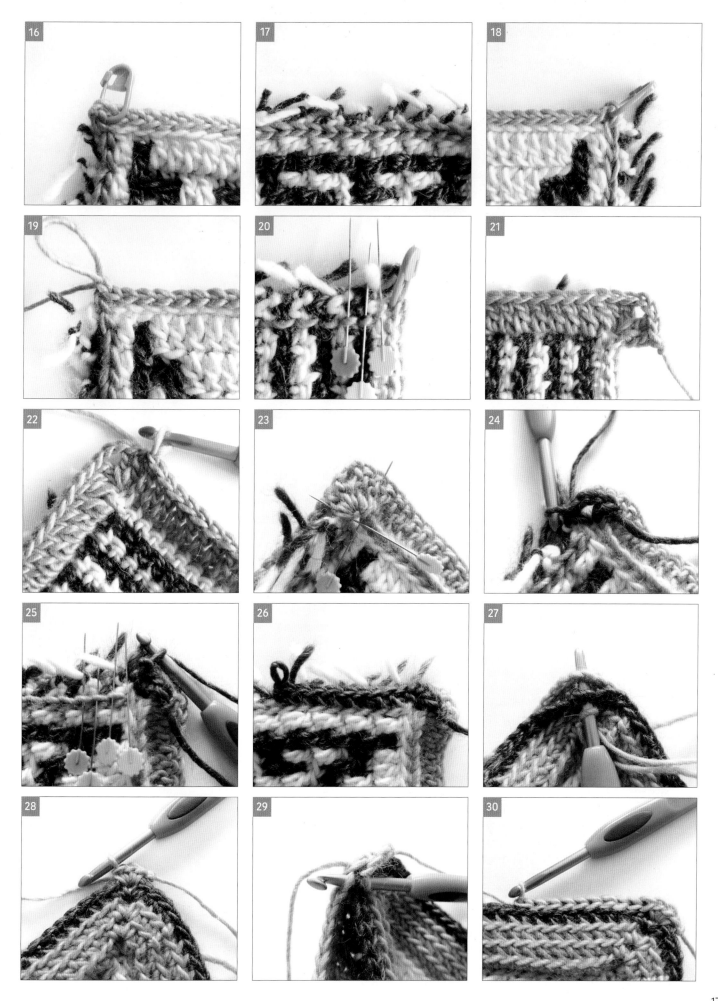

Final Touches

Making A Tassel

Preparation:

1. Cut Card to required size.

2. Cut the required number of long lengths of yarn. *Image 31*

3. Cut the required number of short lengths of yarn.

Method:

1. Holding the longer strands together, wrap them around the card the required number of times. *Image 32*

2. Gently remove wound strands from the card and using one shorter strand, tie it tightly around the center (between the folded yarn loops - looks like a "bow"). Knot it twice to secure, and thread both the tails onto a needle. *Image 33*

3. With right side of blanket facing, insert the needle from back to front through the center sc of the corner 3-sc group. *Image 34*

4. Insert the needle under the knotted strand (to catch the yarn) and insert the needle again into the center sc, but this time from front to back. *Images 35 & 36*

5. Remove the yarn tails from the needle, then thread them one at a time back onto the needle and weave in the ends along either side of the corner. *Image 37*

6. Fold the attached "bow" in half (so the loops are together) and using another shorter strand, wrap it 3 times tightly around the yarn group about ½" (1.25 cm) from the fold. Tie 3 knots at the back of the yarn group to secure. *Image 38*

7. Thread both the tails onto a needle and insert the needle under the strand tied around the yarn group - from top to bottom. The tails are now part of the yarn group. *Image 39*

8. Cut all the folded loops and trim the tassel to desired length. *Image 40*

Making A Fringe

Preparation:

1. Cut Card to required size.

2. Cut the number of yarn lengths required.

Method:

1. Wrap the yarn around the card. *Image 41*

2. Carefully remove the wound yarn from the card. With the right side of the blanket facing, insert hook from back to front in the specified stitch or space and pull the folded strands of yarn halfway through. (The folded strand forms a loop at the back, with the tails and other folds in front.) *Images 42 & 43*

3. Thread the tail end of strands through the back loop. *Image 44*

4. Pull tight to secure.

5. Cut the folds and trim to desired length. *Image 45*

Starting Your Project

Swatching

Before starting any project, it is good practice to work up a swatch (or three!). This little piece of fabric provides a lot of information. From a swatch one can check the gauge (if needed), and working a swatch gives you a "feel" of the yarn you've chosen and how it reacts. Does it split easily? Is it too rough on your hands? Do the colors chosen have enough contrast? At this point, you might want to change your mind and use a different yarn.

A swatch also can determine the "drape" of the fabric – which relates to the hook size used. If you prefer a denser fabric, then make another swatch using a smaller size hook. Similarly, if you want a looser (or fluffier) feel, then try a swatch using a larger size hook. Keep changing your hook size until you get the drape you desire.

For the blankets in this book, you can use one repeat of the pattern to make a swatch. When working your Mosaic swatch, concentrate on training your double crochet stitches, as they should not pull your other stitches' loops.

Do not get stressed with the final swatch measurements. For a blanket, the gauge is not that critical. An extra inch or centimeter more (or less) is not that important. If needed, you can always add or decrease the number of pattern repeats, either in width and/or in length.

To adapt the design, add or delete a multiple of the total number of stitches in the repeat. In the above example, each row has 2 Border Stitches, 2 Extra Stitches, and 5 stitches in the repeat. To increase the width, add multiples of the 5 repeat stitches to maintain the integrity of the design. Therefore a foundation row with two repeats would have 14 stitches = (2x5) + 2 Border Stiches + 2 Extra Stitches. And a foundation row with ninety-two repeats would have 464 stitches = (92x5) + 2 Border Stitches + 2 Extra Stitches.

Once you are happy with the outcome of your swatch, then start your project.

Making A Practice Swatch

If you are new to Mosaic Crochet (or just need a quick refresher course), try working a practice swatch. The chart and the written pattern (with photo tutorial) will give you the same result.

This swatch has 3 stitch pattern repeats. At the end of each row, inside the round brackets there are the counting stitches of the entire row. Inside the square brackets there are the counting stitches of one repeat.

Foundation Row / Row 1 (using Foundation Single Crochet): *(Right Side)* (C1) Make 19 FSC. (19 sc) Cut yarn, leaving a tail. Do not turn your work. Continue with Row 2.

OR

Foundation Row / Row 1 (using Chain foundation): *(Right Side)* (C1) Ch 20, starting in 2nd ch from hook, sc in each ch across. (19 sc) Cut yarn, leaving a tail. Do not turn your work. Continue with Row 2. *Image 1*

Notes:

1. From now on, work all single crochet stitches (except first and last Border Stitch) in back loops only (BLO) and all double crochet stitches in front loops only (FLO).

2. Start each row with a standing single crochet (through both loops) in the first stitch (first Border Stitch). Work a chain stitch after the first Border Stitch.

3. At the end of the row, before the last stitch, make a chain stitch and work a Border Stitch (through both loops) in the last stitch.

Row 2: (C2) BS, ch 1 *(do not skip any sts on foundation row)*, 17 sc, ch 1, *(do not skip any sts)*, BS. (19 sc) *Images 2-7*

Row 3: (C1) BS, ch 1, 2 sc, [1 sc, 2 dc, 2 sc] 3 times, ch 1, BS. (13 sc & 6 dc) [3 sc & 2 dc] *Images 8-13*

Row 4: (C2) BS, ch 1, 1 dc, 1 sc, [1 dc, 2 sc, 1 dc, 1 sc] 3 times, ch 1, BS. (12 sc & 7 dc) [3 sc & 2 dc] *Images 14 & 15*

Row 5: (C1) BS, ch 1, 1 sc, 1 dc, [2 sc, 1 dc, 1 sc, 1 dc] 3 times, ch 1, BS. (12 sc & 7 dc) [3 sc & 2 dc] *Images 16 & 17*

Row 6: (C2) BS, ch 1, 2 sc, [1 sc, 1 dc, 3 sc] 3 times, ch 1, BS. (16 sc & 3 dc) [4 sc & 1 dc] *Images 18 & 19*

Row 7: (C1) BS, ch 1, 1 dc, 1 sc, [1 dc, 2 sc, 1 dc, 1 sc] 3 times, ch 1, BS. (12 sc & 7 dc) [3 sc & 2 dc] *Images 20 & 21*

Row 8: (C2) BS, ch 1, 1 sc, 1 dc, [2 sc, 1 dc, 1 sc, 1 dc] 3 times, ch 1, BS. (12 sc & 7 dc) [3 sc & 2 dc] *Images 22 & 23*

Row 9: (C1) BS, ch 1, 2 sc, [2 dc, 3 sc] 3 times, ch 1, BS. (13 sc & 6 dc) [3 sc & 2 dc] *Images 24 - 26*

Pratice Swatch

BS	5	4	3	2	1	E	E	BS		
				x	x				C1	R9
	x		x				x		C2	R8
		x			x			x	C1	R7
			x						C2	R6
	x		x				x		C1	R5
		x			x			x	C2	R4
			x	x					C1	R3
									C2	R2
									C1	FR/R1

Repeat

☐ sc in BLO	E Extra Stitch
x dc in FLO, 2 rows down	☐ C1
▨ Border Stitch (BS)	▨ C2

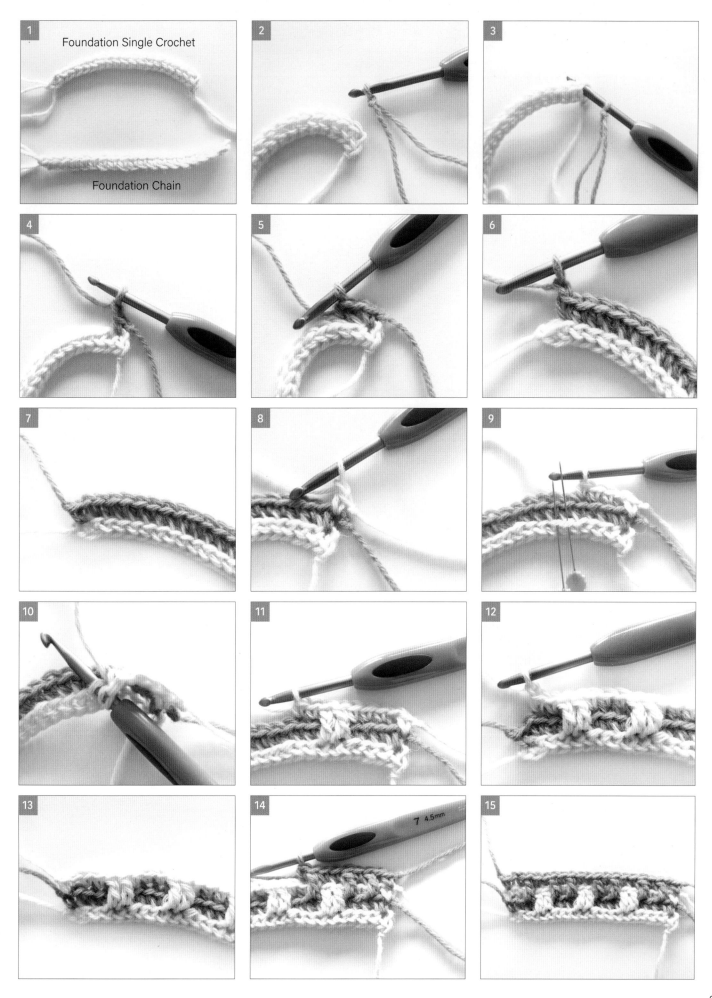

1 Foundation Single Crochet

Foundation Chain

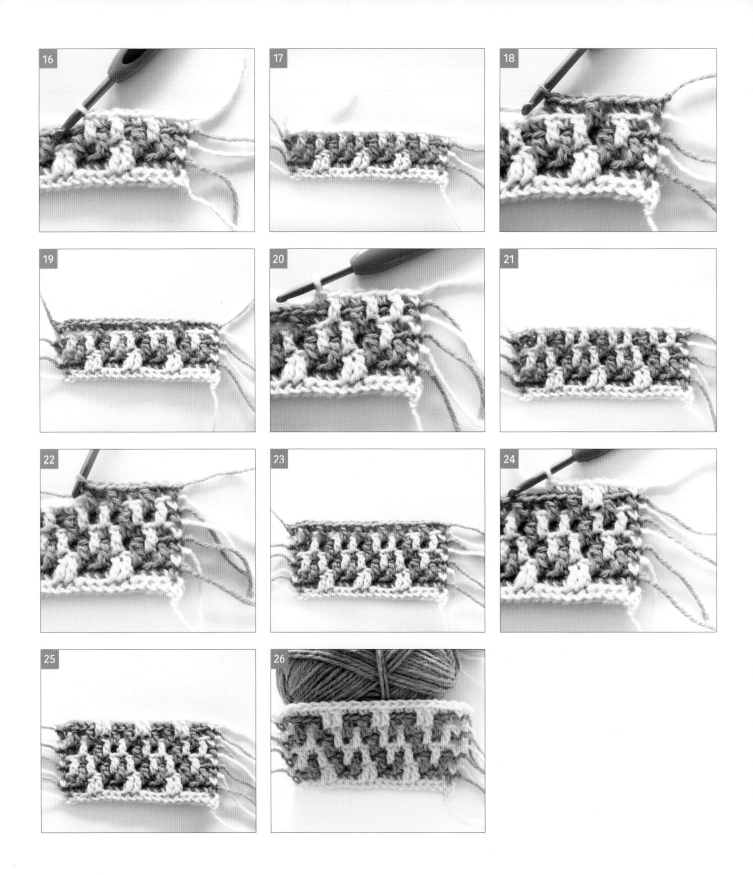

PROJECTS

25

Fluffy
SNOWFLAKES

Materials

DK / Light Weight Yarn

Jody Long Alba (50% Merino Wool, 25% Alpaca, 25% Viscose)

1 ball – 3.52 ounces (382 yards) / 100 grams (350 meters)

Color 1 (C1): Midnight (#010) - 6 balls

Color 2 (C2): Winter (#019) - 5 balls

Color 3 (C3): Moss (#013) - 1 ball

Size G-6 (4.00 mm) Crochet Hook

Scissors and Tapestry Needle

Finished Size & Gauge

Blanket: About 39" (100 cm) wide and 55" (140 cm) long

Gauge: 20 stitches and 20 rows = 4" (10 cm) approximately.

Note: The finished size of the blanket might differ due to the gauge needed for the choice of yarn used. The overall size of the blanket can be customized by adding or removing pattern repeats, which will affect the amount of yarn required.

Multiple (Stitch Pattern Repeat): 46 + 5

There are 46 stitches in each pattern repeat.

The additional 5 stitches are the 2 Border Stitches plus 2 Extra Stitches at the beginning of a row and 1 Extra Stitch at the end of the row.

Pattern Notes:

1 The Blanket pictured has 4 stitch pattern repeats.

2 Refer to General Pattern Notes.

3 See section on Special Stitches, if needed.

Skill Level

Intermediate or Adventurous Beginner

BLANKET

Foundation Row / Row 1: *(Right Side)* (C1) Make 189 FSC. Cut yarn. Do not turn your work. Continue with row 2. (189 sc) Or for Chain Foundation:

Foundation Row / Row 1: *(Right Side)* (C1) Ch 190, starting in 2nd ch from hook, sc in each ch across. Cut yarn, leaving a tail. Do not turn your work. Continue with Row 2.
(189 sc)

Row 2: (C2) BS, ch 1, 187 sc, ch 1, BS. *(189 sc)*

Row 3: (C1) BS, ch 1, 1 dc, 1 sc, [1 dc, 8 sc, (1 dc, 1 sc) 2 times, 2 dc, 1 sc, 4 dc, 5 sc, 4 dc, 1 sc, 2 dc, (1 sc, 1 dc) 2 times, 8 sc, 1 dc, 1 sc] 4 times, 1 dc, ch 1, BS. *(115 sc & 74 dc) [28 sc & 18 dc]*

Repeat Starts:

Row 4: (C2) BS, ch 1, 2 sc, [1 sc, 1 dc, 2 sc, 1 dc, 3 sc, 1 dc, 11 sc, (1 dc, 1 sc) 2 times, 1 dc, 11 sc, 1 dc, 3 sc, (1 dc, 2 sc) 2 times] 4 times, 1 sc, ch 1, BS. *(153 sc & 36 dc) [37 sc & 9 dc]*

Row 5: (C1) BS, ch 1, 1 dc, 1 sc, [(3 sc, 1 dc) 2 times, 2 sc, 3 dc, 1 sc, 4 dc, 3 sc, 1 dc, 1 sc, 1 dc, 3 sc, 4 dc, 1 sc, 3 dc, 2 sc, 1 dc, 3 sc, 1 dc, 4 sc] 4 times, 1 dc, ch 1, BS. *(107 sc & 82 dc) [26 sc & 20 dc]*

Row 6: (C2) BS, ch 1, 1 dc, 1 sc, [2 sc, 1 dc, 3 sc, 1 dc, 2 sc, 1 dc, 8 sc, (1 dc, 3 sc) 2 times, 1 dc, 8 sc, 1 dc, 2 sc, 1 dc, 3 sc, 1 dc, 2 sc, 1 dc] 4 times, 1 sc, ch 1, BS. *(148 sc & 41 dc) [36 sc & 10 dc]*

Row 7: (C1) BS, ch 1, 1 dc, 1 sc, [1 sc, 1 dc, 3 sc, 1 dc, 2 sc, 1 dc, 1 sc, 6 dc, (3 sc, 2 dc) 2 times, 3 sc, 6 dc, 1 sc, 1 dc, 2 sc, 1 dc, 3 sc, 1 dc, 2 sc] 4 times, 1 dc, ch 1, BS. *(99 sc & 90 dc) [24 sc & 22 dc]*

Row 8: (C2) BS, ch 1, 2 sc, [1 dc, 2 sc, 2 dc, 2 sc, 1 dc, 8 sc, 1 dc, 4 sc, 1 dc, 1 sc, 1 dc, 4 sc, 1 dc, 8 sc, 1 dc, 2 sc, 2 dc, 2 sc, 1 dc, 1 sc] 4 times, 1 sc, ch 1, BS. *(141 sc & 48 dc) [34 sc & 12 dc]*

Row 9: (C1) BS, ch 1, 2 sc, [2 sc, 1 dc, 3 sc, 1 dc, 2 sc, 5 dc, 3 sc, 2 dc, 3 sc, 1 dc, 3 sc, 2 dc, 3 sc, 5 dc, 2 sc, 1 dc, 3 sc, 1 dc, 2 sc, 1 dc] 4 times, 1 dc, ch 1, BS. *(106 sc & 83 dc) [26 sc & 20 dc]*

Row 10: (C2) BS, ch 1, 2 sc, [2 dc, 2 sc, 2 dc, 8 sc, 1 dc, 4 sc, 1 dc, 5 sc, 1 dc, 4 sc, 1 dc, 8 sc, 2 dc, 2 sc, 2 dc, 1 sc] 4 times, 1 sc, ch 1, BS. *(141 sc & 48 dc) [34 sc & 12 dc]*

Row 11: (C1) BS, ch 1, 2 dc, [3 sc, 1 dc, 4 sc, 4 dc, 3 sc, 2 dc, 3 sc, 5 dc, 3 sc, 2 dc, 3 sc, 4 dc, 4 sc, 1 dc, 3 sc, 1 dc] 4 times, 1 dc, ch 1, BS. *(106 sc & 83 dc) [26 sc & 20 dc]*

Row 12: (C2) BS, ch 1, 2 sc, [1 sc, 2 dc, 2 sc, 1 dc, 6 sc, 1 dc, 4 sc, 1 dc, 9 sc, 1 dc, 4 sc, 1 dc, 6 sc, 1 dc, 2 sc, 2 dc, 2 sc] 4 times, 1 sc, ch 1, BS. *(149 sc & 40 dc) [36 sc & 10 dc]*

Row 13: (C1) BS, ch 1, 1 dc, 1 sc, [1 dc, 2 sc, 2 dc, 1 sc, 4 dc, 3 sc, 2 dc, 3 sc, 4 dc, 1 sc, 4 dc, 3 sc, 2 dc, 3 sc, 4 dc, 1 sc, 2 dc, 2 sc, 1 dc, 1 sc] 4 times, 1 dc, ch 1, BS. *(83 sc & 106 dc) [20 sc & 26 dc]*

Row 14: (C2) BS, ch 1, 2 sc, [2 sc, 1 dc, 7 sc, 1 dc, 4 sc, 1 dc, 13 sc, 1 dc, 4 sc, 1 dc, 7 sc, 1 dc, 3 sc] 4 times, 1 sc, ch 1, BS. *(165 sc & 24 dc) [40 sc & 6 dc]*

Row 15: (C1) BS, ch 1, 1 dc, 1 sc, [2 dc, 1 sc, 5 dc, 3 sc, 2 dc, 3 sc, 5 dc, 1 sc, 1 dc, 1 sc, 5 dc, 3 sc, 2 dc, 3 sc, 5 dc, 1 sc, 2 dc, 1 sc] 4 times, 1 dc, ch 1, BS. *(71 sc & 118 dc) [17 sc & 29 dc]*

Row 16: (C2) BS, ch 1, 2 sc, [8 sc, 1 dc, 4 sc, 1 dc, 17 sc, 1 dc, 4 sc, 1 dc, 9 sc] 4 times, 1 sc, ch 1, BS. *(173 sc & 16 dc) [42 sc & 4 dc]*

Row 17: (C1) BS, ch 1, 2 dc, [1 sc, 5 dc, 3 sc, 2 dc, 3 sc, 5 dc, (1 sc, 2 dc) 2 times, 1 sc, 5 dc, 3 sc, 2 dc, 3 sc, 5 dc, 1 sc, 1 dc] 4 times, 1 dc, ch 1, BS. *(70 sc & 119 dc) [17 sc & 29 dc]*

Row 18: (C2) BS, ch 1, 2 sc, [6 sc, 1 dc, 4 sc, 1 dc, 7 sc, 1 dc, 5 sc, 1 dc, 7 sc, 1 dc, 4 sc, 1 dc, 7 sc] 4 times, 1 sc, ch 1, BS. *(165 sc & 24 dc) [40 sc & 6 dc]*

Row 19: (C1) BS, ch 1, 1 dc, 1 sc, [4 dc, 3 sc, 2 dc, 3 sc, 4 dc, 1 sc, 2 dc, 2 sc, 1 sc, 1 dc, 2 sc, 2 dc, 1 sc, 4 dc, 3 sc, 2 dc, 3 sc, 4 dc, 1 sc] 4 times, 1 dc, ch 1, BS. *(83 sc & 106 dc) [20 sc & 26 dc]*

Row 20: (C2) BS, ch 1, 2 sc, [(4 sc, 1 dc) 2 times, 6 sc, 1 dc, 2 sc, 2 dc, 3 sc, 2 dc, 2 sc, 1 dc, 6 sc, 1 dc, 4 sc, 1 dc, 5 sc] 4 times, 1 sc, ch 1, BS. *(149 sc & 40 dc) [36 sc & 10 dc]*

Row 21: (C1) BS, ch 1, 2 dc, [(2 dc, 3 sc) 2 times, 4 dc, 4 sc, (1 dc, 3 sc) 2 times, 1 dc, 4 sc, 4 dc, 3 sc, 2 dc, 3 sc, 3 dc] 4 times, 1 dc, ch 1, BS. *(106 sc & 83 dc) [26 sc & 20 dc]*

Row 22: (C2) BS, ch 1, 2 sc, [2 sc, 1 dc, 4 sc, 1 dc, 8 sc, 2 dc, 2 sc, 2 dc, 1 sc, 2 dc, 2 sc, 2 dc, 8 sc, 1 dc, 4 sc, 1 dc, 3 sc] 4 times, 1 sc, ch 1, BS. *(141 sc & 48 dc) [34 sc & 12 dc]*

Row 23: (C1) BS, ch 1, 2 dc, [3 sc, 2 dc, 3 sc, 5 dc, 2 sc, 1 dc, 3 sc, 1 dc, (2 sc, 1 dc) 2 times, 3 sc, 1 dc, 2 sc, 5 dc, 3 sc, 2 dc, 3 sc, 1 dc] 4 times, 1 dc, ch 1, BS. *(106 sc & 83 dc) [26 sc & 20 dc]*

Row 24: (C2) BS, ch 1, 2 sc, [1 dc, 4 sc, 1 dc, 8 sc, 1 dc, 2 sc, 2 dc, 2 sc, 1 dc, 1 sc, 1 dc, 2 sc, 2 dc, 2 sc, 1 dc, 8 sc, 1 dc, 4 sc, 1 dc, 1 sc] 4 times, 1 sc, ch 1, BS. *(141 sc & 48 dc) [34 sc & 12 dc]*

Row 25: (C1) BS, ch 1, 1 dc, 1 sc, [1 sc, 2 dc, 3 sc, 6 dc, 1 sc, 1 dc, 2 sc, 1 dc, (3 sc, 1 dc) 3 times, 2 sc, 1 dc, 1 sc, 6 dc, 3 sc, 2 dc, 2 sc] 4 times, 1 dc, ch 1, BS. *(99 sc & 90 dc) [24 sc & 22 dc]*

Row 26: (C2) BS, ch 1, 1 dc, 1 sc, [3 sc, 1 dc, 8 sc, 1 dc, 2 sc, 1 dc, 3 sc, 1 dc, (2 sc, 1 dc) 2 times, 3 sc, 1 dc, 2 sc, 1 dc, 8 sc, 1 dc, 3 sc, 1 dc] 4 times, 1 sc, ch 1, BS. *(148 sc & 41 dc) [36 sc & 10 dc]*

Row 27: (C1) BS, ch 1, 1 dc, 1 sc, [1 dc, 3 sc, 4 dc, 1 sc, 3 dc, 2 sc, 1 dc, 3 sc, 1 dc, 7 sc, 1 dc, 3 sc, 1 dc, 2 sc, 3 dc, 1 sc, 4 dc, 3 sc, 1 dc, 1 sc] 4 times, 1 dc, ch 1, BS. *(107 sc & 82 dc) [26 sc & 20 dc]*

Row 28: (C2) BS, ch 1, 1 dc, 1 sc, [1 sc, 1 dc, 11 sc, (1 dc, 3 sc, 1 dc, 2 sc) 2 times, 1 dc, 3 sc, 1 dc, 11 sc, 1 dc, 1 sc, 1 dc] 4 times, 1 sc, ch 1, BS. *(152 sc & 37 dc) [37 sc & 9 dc]*

Row 29: (C1) BS, ch 1, 1 dc, 1 sc, [2 sc, 4 dc, 1 sc, 2 dc, (1 sc, 1 dc) 2 times (8 sc, 1 dc, 1 sc, 1 dc) 2 times, 1 sc, 2 dc, 1 sc, 4 dc, 3 sc] 4 times, 1 dc, ch 1, BS. *(115 sc & 74 dc) [28 sc & 18 dc]*

Row 30: (C2) BS, ch 1, 1 dc, 1 sc, [1 sc, 1 dc, 11 sc, (1 dc, 3 sc, 1 dc, 2 sc) 2 times, 1 dc, 3 sc, 1 dc, 11 sc, 1 dc, 1 sc, 1 dc] 4 times, 1 sc, ch 1, BS. *(152 sc & 37 dc) [37 sc & 9 dc]*

Row 31: (C1) BS, ch 1, 1 dc, 1 sc, [1 dc, 3 sc, 4 dc, 1 sc, 3 dc, 2 sc, 1 dc, 3 sc, 1 dc, 7 sc, 1 dc, 3 sc, 1 dc, 2 sc, 3 dc, 1 sc, 4 dc, 3 sc, 1 dc, 1 sc] 4 times, 1 dc, ch 1, BS. *(107 sc & 82 dc) [26 sc & 20 dc]*

Row 32: (C2) BS, ch 1, 1 dc, 1 sc, [3 sc, 1 dc, 8 sc, 1 dc, 2 sc, 1 dc, 3 sc, (1 dc, 2 sc) 2 times, 1 dc, 3 sc, 1 dc, 2 sc, 1 dc, 8 sc, 1 dc, 3 sc, 1 dc] 4 times, 1 sc, ch 1, BS. *(148 sc & 41 dc) [36 sc & 10 dc]*

Row 33: (C1) BS, ch 1, 1 dc, 1 sc, [1 sc, 2 dc, 3 sc, 6 dc, 1 sc, 1 dc, 2 sc, (1 dc, 3 sc) 3 times, 1 dc, 2 sc, 1 dc, 1 sc, 6 dc, 3 sc, 2 dc, 2 sc] 4 times, 1 dc, ch 1, BS. *(99 sc & 90 dc) [24 sc & 22 dc]*

Row 34: (C2) BS, ch 1, 2 sc, [1 dc, 4 sc, 1 dc, 8 sc, 1 dc, 2 sc, 2 dc, 2 sc, 1 dc, 1 sc, 1 dc, 2 sc, 2 dc, 2 sc, 1 dc, 8 sc, 1 dc, 4 sc, 1 dc, 1 sc] 4 times, 1 sc, ch 1, BS. *(141 sc & 48 dc) [34 sc & 12 dc]*

Row 35: (C1) BS, ch 1, 2 dc, [3 sc, 2 dc, 3 sc, 5 dc, 2 sc, 1 dc, 3 sc, (1 dc, 2 sc) 2 times, 1 dc, 3 sc, 1 dc, 2 sc, 5 dc, 3 sc, 2 dc, 3 sc, 1 dc] 4 times, 1 dc, ch 1, BS. *(106 sc & 83 dc) [26 sc & 20 dc]*

Row 36: (C2) BS, ch 1, 2 sc, [2 sc, 1 dc, 4 sc, 1 dc, 8 sc, 2 dc, 2 sc, 2 dc, 1 sc, 2 dc, 2 sc, 2 dc, 8 sc, 1 dc, 4 sc, 1 dc, 3 sc] 4 times, 1 sc, ch 1, BS. *(141 sc & 48 dc) [34 sc & 12 dc]*

Row 37: (C1) BS, ch 1, 2 dc, [(2 dc, 3 sc) 2 times, 4 dc, 4 sc, (1 dc, 3 sc) 2 times, 1 dc, 4 sc, 4 dc, 3 sc, 2 dc, 3 sc, 3 dc] 4 times, 1 dc, ch 1, BS. *(106 sc & 83 dc) [26 sc & 20 dc]*

Row 38: (C2) BS, ch 1, 2 sc, [(4 sc, 1 dc) 2 times, 6 sc, 1 dc, 2 sc, 2 dc, 3 sc, 2 dc, 2 sc, 1 dc, 6 sc, 1 dc, 4 sc, 1 dc, 5 sc] 4 times, 1 sc, ch 1, BS. *(149 sc & 40 dc) [36 sc & 10 dc]*

Row 39: (C1) BS, ch 1, 1 dc, 1 sc, [4 dc, 3 sc, 2 dc, 3 sc, 4 dc, 1 sc, 2 dc, 2 sc, 1 dc, 1 sc, 1 dc, 2 sc, 2 dc, 1 sc, 4 dc, 3 sc, 2 dc, 3 sc, 4 dc, 1 sc] 4 times, 1 dc, ch 1, BS. *(83 sc & 106 dc) [20 sc & 26 dc]*

Row 40: (C2) BS, ch 1, 2 sc, [6 sc, 1 dc, 4 sc, 1 dc, 7 sc, 1 dc, 5 sc, 1 dc, 7 sc, 1 dc, 4 sc, 1 dc, 7 sc] 4 times, 1 sc, ch 1, BS. *(165 sc & 24 dc) [40 sc & 6 dc]*

Row 41: (C1) BS, ch 1, 2 dc, [1 sc, 5 dc, 3 sc, 2 dc, 3 sc, 5 dc, (1 sc, 2 dc) 2 times, 1 dc, 5 dc, 3 sc, 2 dc, 3 sc, 5 dc, 1 sc, 1 dc] 4 times, 1 dc, ch 1, BS. *(70 sc & 119 dc) [17 sc & 29 dc]*

Row 42: (C2) BS, ch 1, 2 sc, [8 sc, 1 dc, 4 sc, 1 dc, 17 sc, 1 dc, 4 sc, 1 dc, 9 sc] 4 times, 1 sc, ch 1, BS. *(173 sc & 16 dc) [42 sc & 4 dc]*

Row 43: (C1) BS, ch 1, 1 dc, 1 sc, [2 dc, 1 sc, 5 dc, 3 sc, 2 dc, 3 sc, 5 dc, 1 sc, 1 sc, 5 dc, 3 sc, 2 dc, 3 sc, 5 dc, 1 sc, 2 dc, 1 sc] 4 times, 1 dc, ch 1, BS. *(71 sc & 118 dc) [17 sc & 29 dc]*

Row 44: (C2) BS, ch 1, 2 sc, [2 sc, 1 dc, 7 sc, 1 dc, 4 sc, 1 dc, 13 sc, 1 dc, 4 sc, 1 dc, 7 sc, 1 dc, 3 sc] 4 times, 1 sc, ch 1, BS. *(165 sc & 24 dc) [40 sc & 6 dc]*

Row 45: (C1) BS, ch 1, 1 dc, 1 sc, [1 dc, 2 sc, 2 dc, 1 sc, 4 dc, 3 sc, 2 dc, 3 sc, 4 dc, 1 sc, 4 dc, 3 sc, 2 dc, 3 sc, 4 dc, 1 sc, 2 dc, 2 sc, 1 dc, 1 sc] 4 times, 1 dc, ch 1, BS. *(83 sc & 106 dc) [20 sc & 26 dc]*

Row 46: (C2) BS, ch 1, 2 sc, [1 sc, 2 dc, 2 sc, 1 dc, 6 sc, 1 dc, 4 sc, 1 dc, 9 sc, 1 dc, 4 sc, 1 dc, 6 sc, 1 dc, 2 sc, 2 dc, 2 sc] 4 times, 1 sc, ch 1, BS. *(149 sc & 40 dc) [36 sc & 10 dc]*

Row 47: (C1) BS, ch 1, 2 dc, [3 sc, 1 dc, 4 sc, 4 dc, 3 sc, 2 dc, 3 sc, 5 dc, 3 sc, 2 dc, 3 sc, 4 dc, 4 sc, 1 dc, 3 sc, 1 dc] 4 times, 1 dc, ch 1, BS. *(106 sc & 83 dc) [26 sc & 20 dc]*

Row 48: (C2) BS, ch 1, 2 sc, [2 dc, 2 sc, 2 dc, 8 sc, 1 dc, 4 sc, 1 dc, 5 sc, 1 dc, 4 sc, 1 dc, 8 sc, 2 dc, 2 sc, 2 dc, 1 sc] 4 times, 1 sc, ch 1, BS. *(141 sc & 48 dc) [34 sc & 12 dc]*

Row 49: (C1) BS, ch 1, 2 dc, [2 sc, 1 dc, 3 sc, 1 dc, 2 sc, 5 dc, 3 sc, 2 dc, 3 sc, 1 dc, 3 sc, 2 dc, 3 sc, 5 dc, 2 sc, 1 dc, 3 sc, 1 dc, 2 sc, 1 dc] 4 times, 1 dc, ch 1, BS. *(106 sc & 83 dc) [26 sc & 20 dc]*

Row 50: (C2) BS, ch 1, 2 sc, [1 dc, 2 sc, 2 dc, 2 sc, 1 dc, 8 sc, 1 dc, 4 sc, 1 sc, 1 dc, 4 sc, 1 dc, 8 sc, 1 dc, 2 sc, 2 dc, 2 sc, 1 dc, 1 sc] 4 times, 1 sc, ch 1, BS. *(141 sc & 48 dc) [34 sc & 12 dc]*

Row 51: (C1) BS, ch 1, 1 dc, 1 sc, [1 sc, 1 dc, 3 sc, 1 dc, 2 sc, 1 dc, 1 sc, 6 dc, (3 sc, 2 dc) 2 times, 3 sc, 6 dc, 1 sc, 1 dc, 2 sc, 1 dc, 3 sc, 1 dc, 2 sc] 4 times, 1 dc, ch 1, BS. *(99 sc & 90 dc) [24 sc & 22 dc]*

Row 52: (C2) BS, ch 1, 1 sc, 1 dc, [2 sc, 1 dc, 3 sc, 1 dc, 2 sc, 1 dc, 8 sc, (1 dc, 3 sc) 2 times, 1 dc, 8 sc, 1 dc, 2 sc, 1 dc, 3 sc, 1 dc, 2 sc, 1 dc] 4 times, 1 sc, ch 1, BS. *(148 sc & 41 dc) [36 sc & 10 dc]*

Row 53: (C1) BS, ch 1, 1 dc, 1 sc, [(3 sc, 1 dc) 2 times, 2 sc, 3 dc, 1 sc, 4 dc, 3 sc, 1 dc, 1 sc, 1 dc, 3 sc, 4 dc, 1 sc, 3 dc, 2 sc, 1 dc, 3 sc, 1 dc, 4 sc] 4 times, 1 dc, ch 1, BS. *(107 sc & 82 dc) [26 sc & 20 dc]*

Row 54: (C2) BS, ch 1, 2 sc, [1 sc, 1 dc, 2 sc, 1 dc, 3 sc, 1 dc, 11 sc, (1 dc, 1 sc) 2 times, 1 dc, 11 sc, 1 dc, 3 sc, (1 dc, 2 sc) 2 times] 4 times, 1 sc, ch 1, BS. *(153 sc & 36 dc) [37 sc & 9 dc]*

Row 55: (C1) BS, ch 1, 1 dc, 1 sc, [1 dc, 8 sc, (1 dc, 1 sc) 2 times, 2 dc, 1 sc, 4 dc, 5 sc, 4 dc, 1 sc, 2 dc, (1 sc, 1 dc) 2 times, 8 sc, 1 dc, 1 sc] 4 times, 1 dc, ch 1, BS. *(115 sc & 74 dc) [28 sc & 18 dc]*

Rows 56-263: Repeat Rows 4-55 *(52 rows)* four times more.

BORDER

Follow instructions for Making the Border.

1. Secure the Yarn Tails.

2. Special Round: With right side facing and C3, join with standing sl st in first st on Foundation Row/Row 1; sl st around, working ch 2 in corners; join with sl st to first ch-2 sp. Cut yarn. *(189 sl sts across top and bottom edges, 263 sl sts across right and left edges & 4 corner ch-2 sps)*

3. Back Layer:

Rnd 1: With wrong side facing and C3, join with standing dc in any corner ch-2 sp on bottom edge; (dc, ch 2, 2 dc) in same sp; dc in each st around *(taking care not to skip the sts before and after ch-2 corner sps)*, working (2 dc, ch 2, 2 dc) in each corner ch-2 sp; join with sl st to first *(standing)* dc. Cut yarn. *(193 dc across short sides, 267 dc across long sides & 4 corner ch-2 sps)*

4. Front Layer:

Rnd 1: With right side facing and C3, join with standing sc in any corner ch-2 sp *(before dc-sts)*, ch 2, sc in same sp *(after the dc-sts)*, working in BLO of sl sts, sc in each st around, working (sc, ch 2, sc) in each corner; join with sl st to first sc. Do NOT cut yarn. *(191 sc across short sides, 265 sc across long sides & 4 corner ch-2 sps)*

Rnd 2: Ch 1, sc in BLO of same st as joining, (sc, ch 2, sc) in next corner ch-2 sp, working in BLO *(except corners)*, sc in each st around, working (sc, ch 2, sc) in corner ch-2 sps; join with sl st to first sc. Cut yarn. *(193 sc across short sides, 267 sc across long sides & 4 corner ch-2 sps)*

5. Join Front & Back Layers

Notes:

a. The entire round is worked through the BLO of both the Front Layer and the corresponding Back Layer stitches together.

b. Corners are worked through the corresponding ch-2 spaces on both layers.

Joining Round: With right side facing and C3, join with standing sc in any corner ch-2 sp, 2 sc in same sp; working in BLO, sl st in each st around, working 3 sc in each corner ch-2 sp; join with sl st to first sc. Cut yarn and sew in all ends.

(193 sl sts across short sides, 267 sl sts across long sides & 4 corner 3-sc)

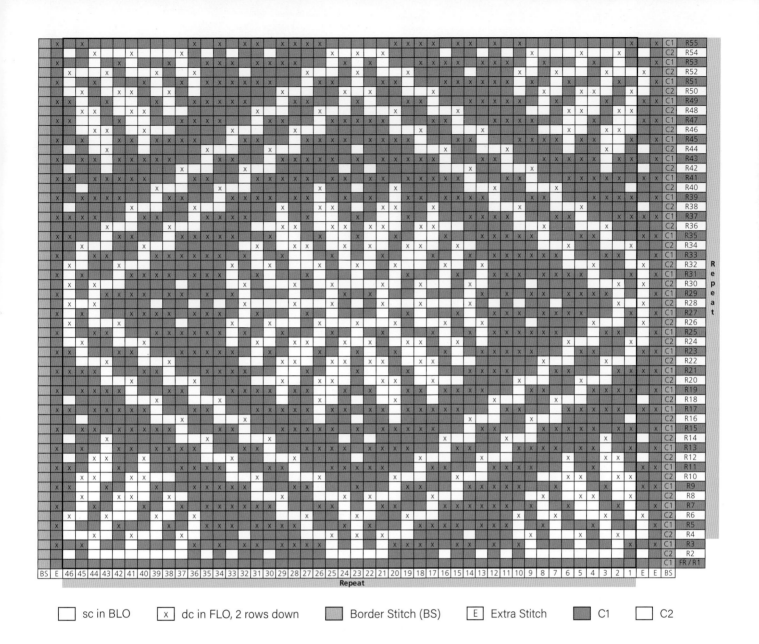

| | | sc in BLO | | x | dc in FLO, 2 rows down | | | Border Stitch (BS) | | E | Extra Stitch | | | C1 | | | C2 |

Wrong side

About 39" (100 cm) wide and 55" (140 cm) long

Chocolate
GEMS

Materials

DK / Light Weight Yarn

Queensland Walkabout (100% Wool)

1 ball - 1.76 oz (157 yards) / 50 g (144 m)

Color 1 (C1): Donkey (#07) – 12 balls

Color 2 (C2): Ivory (#12) – 11 balls

Size I-9 (5.5 mm) crochet hook (Blanket body and Special Round of the Border)

Size H-8 (5 mm) crochet hook (Front and Back Layers of the Border)

Scissors and Tapestry Needle

Finished Size & Gauge

Blanket: About 37" (93 cm) wide and 52" (132 cm) long.
Gauge: 17 stitches and 17 rows = 4" (10 cm) approximately.

Note: The finished size of the blanket might differ due to the gauge needed for the choice of yarn used. The overall size of the blanket can be customized by adding or removing pattern repeats, which will affect the amount of yarn required.

Multiple (Stitch Pattern Repeat): 12 + 5

There are 12 stitches in each pattern repeat.
The additional 5 stitches are the 2 Border Stitches plus 2 Extra Stitches at the beginning of a row and 1 Extra Stitch at the end of the row.

Pattern Notes

1 The Blanket pictured has 12 stitch pattern repeats.

2 Refer to General Pattern Notes.

3 See section on Special Stitches, if needed.

Skill Level
Intermediate or Adventurous Beginner

BLANKET

Foundation Row / Row 1: *(Right Side)* (C1) Using larger hook, make 149 FSC. Cut yarn. Do not turn your work. Continue with row 2. *(149 sc)*

Or for Chain Foundation:

Foundation Row / Row 1: *(Right Side)* (C1) Using larger hook, ch 150, starting in 2nd ch from hook, sc in each ch across. Cut yarn, leaving a tail. Do not turn your work. Continue with Row 2. *(149 sc)*

Row 2: (C2) BS, ch 1, 147 sc, ch 1, BS. *(149 sc)*

Row 3: (C1) BS, ch 1, 2 dc, [(2 sc, 1 dc) 4 times] 12 times, 1 dc, ch 1, BS. *(98 sc & 51 dc) [8 sc & 4 dc]*

Row 4: (C2) BS, ch 1, 2 sc, [(1 dc, 3 sc, 1 dc, 1 sc) 2 times] 12 times, 1 sc, ch 1, BS. *(101 sc & 48 dc) [8 sc & 4 dc]*

Row 5: (C1) BS, ch 1, 2 dc, [(1 sc, 1 dc) 6 times] 12 times, 1 dc, ch 1, BS. *(74 sc & 75 dc) [6 sc & 6 dc]*

Row 6: (C2) BS, ch 1, 2 sc, [(1 dc, 3 sc, 1 dc, 1 sc) 2 times] 12 times, 1 sc, ch 1, BS. *(101 sc & 48 dc) [8 sc & 4 dc]*

Row 7: (C1) BS, ch 1, 2 dc, [(2 sc, 1 dc) 4 times] 12 times, 1 dc, ch 1, BS. *(98 sc & 51 dc) [8 sc & 4 dc]*

Row 8: (C2) BS, ch 1, 2 sc, [(2 dc, 1 sc) 4 times] 12 times, 1 sc, ch 1, BS. *(53 sc & 96 dc) [4 sc & 8 dc]*

Row 9: (C1) BS, ch 1, 2 dc, [(5 sc, 1 dc) 2 times] 12 times, 1 dc, ch 1, BS. *[122 sc & 27 dc] [10 sc & 2 dc]*

Row 10: (C2) BS, ch 1, 2 sc, [1 sc, 3 dc, 3 sc, 3 dc, 2 sc] 12 times, 1 sc, ch 1, BS. *(77 sc & 72 dc) [6 sc & 6 dc]*

Row 11: (C1) BS, ch 1, 1 dc, 1 sc, [(1 dc, 3 sc, 1 dc, 1 sc) 2 times] 12 times, 1 dc, ch 1, BS. *(99 sc & 50 dc) [8 sc & 4 dc]*

Row 12: (C2) BS, ch 1, 2 sc, [2 sc, (2 dc, 3 sc) 2 times] 12 times, 1 sc, ch 1, BS. *(101 sc & 48 dc) [8 sc & 4 dc]*

Row 13: (C1) BS, ch 1, 2 dc, [1 sc, 1 dc, (3 sc, 1 dc) 2 times, 1 sc, 1 dc] 12 times, 1 dc, ch 1, BS. *(98 sc & 51 dc) [8 sc & 4 dc]*

Row 14: (C2) BS, ch 1, 2 sc, [3 sc, 2 dc, 1 sc, 2 dc, 4 sc] 12 times, 1 sc, ch 1, BS. *(101 sc & 48 dc) [8 sc & 4 dc]*

Row 15: (C1) BS, ch 1, 1 dc, 1 sc, [1 dc, 1 sc, 1 dc, 5 sc, (1 dc, 1 sc) 2 times] 12 times, 1 dc, ch 1, BS. *(99 sc & 50 dc) [8 sc & 4 dc]*

Row 16: (C2) BS, ch 1, 2 sc, [1 sc, 1 dc, 2 sc, 3 dc, 2 sc, 1 dc, 2 sc] 12 times, 1 sc, ch 1, BS. *(89 sc & 60 dc) [7 sc & 5 dc]*

Row 17: (C1) BS, ch 1, 2 dc, [(3 sc, 1 dc) 3 times] 12 times, 1 dc, ch 1, BS. *(110 sc & 39 dc) [9 sc & 3 dc]*

Row 18: (C2) BS, ch 1, 2 sc, [1 dc, 1 sc, (1 dc, 2 sc) 2 times, (1 dc, 1 sc) 2 times] 12 times, 1 sc, ch 1, BS. *(89 sc & 60 dc) [7 sc & 5 dc]*

Row 19: (C1) BS, ch 1, 1 dc, 1 sc, [4 sc, 1 dc, 1 sc, 1 dc, 5 sc] 12 times, 1 dc, ch 1, BS. *(123 sc & 26 dc) [10 sc & 2 dc]*

Row 20: (C2) BS, ch 1, 2 sc, [1 dc, 1 sc, (1 dc, 2 sc) 2 times, (1 dc, 1 sc) 2 times] 12 times, 1 sc, ch 1, BS. *(89 sc & 60 dc) [7 sc & 5 dc]*

Repeat Begins:

Row 21: (C1) BS, ch 1, 1 dc, 1 sc, [(3 sc, 1 dc) 2 times, 4 sc] 12 times, 1 dc, ch 1, BS. *(123 sc & 26 dc) [10 sc & 2 dc]*

Row 22: (C2) BS, ch 1, 1 sc, 1 dc, [(1 sc, 1 dc, 2 sc, 1 dc) 2 times, 1 sc, 1 dc] 12 times, 1 sc, ch 1, BS. *(88 sc & 61 dc) [7 sc & 5 dc]*

Row 23: (C1) BS, ch 1, 1 dc, 1 sc, [(2 sc, 1 dc) 3 times, 3 sc] 12 times, 1 dc, ch 1, BS. *(111 sc & 38 dc) [9 sc & 3 dc]*

Row 24: (C2) BS, ch 1, 2 sc, [1 dc, 2 sc, 1 dc, 3 sc, 1 dc, 2 sc, 1 dc, 1 sc] 12 times, 1 sc, ch 1, BS. *(101 sc & 48 dc) [8 sc & 4 dc]*

Row 25: (C1) BS, ch 1, 1 dc, 1 sc, [1 sc, 1 dc, 2 sc, 1 dc, 1 sc, (1 dc, 2 sc) 2 times] 12 times, 1 sc, ch 1, BS. *(99 sc & 50 dc) [8 sc & 4 dc]*

Row 26: (C2) BS, ch 1, 1 dc, 1 sc, [2 sc, 1 dc, 5 sc, 1 dc, 2 sc, 1 dc] 12 times, 1 sc, ch 1, BS. *(112 sc & 37 dc) [9 sc & 3 dc]*

Row 27: (C1) BS, ch 1, 1 dc, 1 sc, [1 dc, 2 sc, (1 dc, 1 sc) 2 times, 1 dc, 2 sc, 1 dc, 1 sc] 12 times, 1 dc, ch 1, BS. *(87 sc & 62 dc) [7 sc & 5 dc]*

Row 28: (C2) BS, ch 1, 2 sc, [1 sc, 1 dc, 7 sc, 1 dc, 2 sc] 12 times, 1 sc, ch 1, BS. *(125 sc & 24 dc) [10 sc & 2 dc]*

Row 29: (C1) BS, ch 1, 2 dc, [2 sc, (1 dc, 1 sc) 3 times, 1 dc, 2 sc, 1 dc] 12 times, 1 dc, ch 1, BS. *(86 sc & 63 dc) [7 sc & 5 dc]*

Row 30: (C2) BS, ch 1, 2 sc, [1 dc, 2 sc, 1 dc, 3 sc, 1 dc, 2 sc, 1 dc, 1 sc] 12 times, 1 sc, ch 1, BS. *(101 sc & 48 dc) [8 sc & 4 dc]*

Row 31: (C1) BS, ch 1, 1 dc, 1 sc, [1 sc, (1 dc, 3 sc) 2 times, 1 dc, 2 sc] 12 times, 1 dc, ch 1, BS. *(111 sc & 38 dc) [9 sc & 3 dc]*

Row 32: (C2) BS, ch 1, 1 dc, 1 sc, [2 sc, (1 dc, 1 sc) 3 times, 1 dc, 2 sc, 1 dc] 12 times, 1 sc, ch 1, BS. *(88 sc & 61 dc) [7 sc & 5 dc]*

Row 33: (C1) BS, ch 1, 1 dc, 1 sc, [1 dc, 9 sc, 1 dc, 1 sc] 12 times, 1 dc, ch 1, BS. *(123 sc & 26 dc) [10 sc & 2 dc]*

Row 34: (C2) BS, ch 1, 1 dc, 1 sc, [2 sc, (1 dc, 1 sc) 3 times, 1 dc, 2 sc, 1 dc] 12 times, 1 sc, ch 1, BS. *(88 sc & 61 dc) [7 sc & 5 dc]*

Row 35: (C1) BS, ch 1, 1 dc, 1 sc, [1 sc, 1 dc, 7 sc, 1 dc, 2 sc] 12 times, 1 dc, ch 1, BS. *(123 sc & 26 dc) [10 sc & 2 dc]*

Row 36: (C2) BS, ch 1, 2 sc, [1 dc, 2 sc, (1 dc, 1 sc) 2 times, 1 dc, 2 sc, 1 dc, 1 sc] 12 times, 1 sc, ch 1, BS. *(89 sc & 60 dc) [7 sc & 5 dc]*

Row 37: (C1) BS, ch 1, 2 dc, [2 sc, 1 dc, 5 sc, 1 dc, 2 sc, 1 dc] 12 times, 1 dc, ch 1, BS. *(110 sc & 39 dc) [9 sc & 3 dc]*

Row 38: (C2) BS, ch 1, 2 sc, [(1 sc, 1 dc, 2 sc, 1 dc) 2 times, 2 sc] 12 times, 1 sc, ch 1, BS. *(101 sc & 48 dc) [8 sc & 4 dc]*

Row 39: (C1) BS, ch 1, 1 dc, 1 sc, [1 dc, 2 sc, 1 dc, 3 sc, 1 dc, 2 sc, 1 dc, 1 sc] 12 times, 1 dc, ch 1, BS. *(99 sc & 50 dc) [8 sc & 4 dc]*

Row 40: (C2) BS, ch 1, 2 sc, [(2 sc, 1 dc) 3 times, 3 sc] 12 times, 1 sc, ch 1, BS. *(113 sc & 36 dc) [9 sc & 3 dc]*

Row 41: (C1) BS, ch 1, 2 dc, [(1 sc, 1 dc, 2 sc, 1 dc) 2 times, 1 sc, 1 dc] 12 times, 1 dc, ch 1, BS. *(86 sc & 63 dc) [7 sc & 5 dc]*

Row 42: (C2) BS, ch 1, 2 sc, [(3 sc, 1 dc) 2 times, 4 sc] 12 times, 1 sc, ch 1, BS. *(125 sc & 24 dc) [10 sc & 2 dc]*

Row 43: (C1) BS, ch 1, 1 dc, 1 sc, [1 dc, 1 sc, (1 dc, 2 sc) 2 times, (1 dc, 1 sc) 2 times] 12 times, 1 dc, ch 1, BS. *(87 sc & 62 dc) [7 sc & 5 dc]*

Row 44: (C2) BS, ch 1, 2 sc, [(1 sc, 1 dc, 2 sc, 1 dc) 2 times, 2 sc] 12 times, 1 sc, ch 1, BS. *(101 sc & 48 dc) [8 sc & 4 dc]*

Row 45: (C1) BS, ch 1, 2 dc, [(3 sc, 1 dc) 3 times] 12 times, 1 dc, ch 1, BS. *(110 sc & 39 dc) [9 sc & 3 dc]*

Row 46: (C2) BS, ch 1, 2 sc, [1 dc, 1 sc, (1 dc, 2 sc) 2 times, (1 dc, 1 sc) 2 times] 12 times, 1 sc, ch 1, BS. *(89 sc & 60 dc) [7 sc & 5 dc]*

Row 47: (C1) BS, ch 1, 1 dc, 1 sc, [4 sc, 1 dc, 1 sc, 1 dc, 5 sc] 12 times, 1 dc, ch 1, BS. *(123 sc & 26 dc) [10 sc & 2 dc]*

Row 48: (C2) BS, ch 1, 2 sc, [1 dc, 1 sc, (1 dc, 2 sc) 2 times, (1 dc, 1 sc) 2 times] 12 times, 1 sc, ch 1, BS. *(89 sc & 60 dc) [7 sc & 5 dc]*

Rows 49-188: Repeat Rows 21-48 *(28 rows)* five times more.

Row 189: (C1) BS, ch 1, 1 dc, 1 sc, [(3 sc, 1 dc) 2 times, 4 sc] 12 times, 1 dc, ch 1, BS. *(123 sc & 26 dc) [10 sc & 2 dc]*

Row 190: (C2) BS, ch 1, 1 sc, 1 dc, [1 sc, 1 dc, 2 sc, 3 dc, 2 sc, 1 dc, 1 sc, 1 dc] 12 times, 1 sc, ch 1, BS. *(76 sc & 73 dc) [6 sc & 6 dc]*

Row 191: (C1) BS, ch 1, 1 dc, 1 sc, [2 sc, 1 dc, 5 dc, 1 dc, 3 sc] 12 times, 1 dc, ch 1, BS. *(123 sc & 26 dc) [10 sc & 2 dc]*

Row 192: (C2) BS, ch 1, 2 sc, [1 dc, 2 sc, 2 dc, 1 sc, 2 dc, 2 sc, 1 dc, 1 sc] 12 times, 1 sc, ch 1, BS. *(77 sc & 72 dc) [6 sc & 6 dc]*

Row 193: (C1) BS, ch 1, 1 dc, 1 sc, [1 sc, 1 dc, (3 sc, 1 dc) 2 times, 2 sc] 12 times, 1 dc, ch 1, BS. *(111 sc & 38 dc) [9 sc & 3 dc]*

Row 194: (C2) BS, ch 1, 1 sc, 1 dc, [2 sc, 2 dc, 3 sc, 2 dc, 2 sc, 1 dc] 12 times, 1 sc, ch 1, BS. *(88 sc & 61 dc) [7 sc & 5 dc]*

Row 195: (C1) BS, ch 1, 1 dc, 1 sc, [(1 dc, 3 sc, 1 dc, 1 sc) 2 times] 12 times, 1 dc, ch 1, BS. *(99 sc & 50 dc) [8 sc & 4 dc]*

Row 196: (C2) BS, ch 1, 2 sc, [1 sc, 3 dc, 3 sc, 3 dc, 2 sc] 12 times, 1 sc, ch 1, BS. *(77 sc & 72 dc) [6 sc & 6 dc]*

Row 197: (C1) BS, ch 1, 2 dc, [(5 sc, 1 dc) 2 times] 12 times, 1 dc, ch 1, BS. *(122 sc & 27 dc) [10 sc & 2 dc]*

Row 198: (C2) BS, ch 1, 2 sc, [(2 dc, 1 sc) 4 times] 12 times, 1 sc, ch 1, BS. *(53 sc & 96 dc) [4 sc & 8 dc]*

Row 199: (C1) BS, ch 1, 2 dc, [(2 sc, 1 dc) 4 times] 12 times, 1 dc, ch 1, BS. *(98 sc & 51 dc) [8 sc & 4 dc]*

Row 200: (C2) BS, ch 1, 2 sc, [(1 dc, 3 sc, 1 dc, 1 sc) 2 times] 12 times, 1 sc, ch 1, BS. *(101 sc & 48 dc) [8 sc & 4 dc]*

Row 201: (C1) BS, ch 1, 2 dc, [(1 sc, 1 dc) 6 times] 12 times, 1 dc, ch 1, BS. *(74 sc & 75 dc) [6 sc & 6 dc]*

Row 202: (C2) BS, ch 1, 2 sc, [(1 dc, 3 sc, 1 dc, 1 sc) 2 times] 12 times, 1 sc, ch 1, BS. *(101 sc & 48 dc) [8 sc & 4 dc]*

Row 203: (C1) BS, ch 1, 2 dc, [(2 sc, 1 dc) 4 times] 12 times, 1 dc, ch 1, BS. *(98 sc & 51 dc) [8 sc & 4 dc]*

BORDER

Follow instructions for Making the Border.

1. Secure the Yarn Tails.

2. Special Round: With right side facing, using larger hook, join C2 with standing sl st in first st on Foundation Row/Row 1; sl st around, working ch 2 in corners; join with sl st to first ch-2 sp. Cut yarn. *(149 sl sts across top and bottom edges, 203 sl sts across right and left edges & 4 corner ch-2 sps)*

3. Back Layer:

Rnd 1: With wrong side facing, using smaller hook, join C1 with standing dc in any corner ch-2 sp on bottom edge; (dc, ch 2, 2 dc) in same sp; dc in each st around *(taking care not to skip the sts before and after ch-2 corner sps)*, working (2 dc, ch 2, 2 dc) in each corner ch-2 sp; join with sl st to first *(standing)* dc. Do NOT cut yarn. *(153 dc across short sides, 207 dc across long sides & 4 corner ch-2 sps)*

Rnd 2: (C1) Ch 3 *(counts as first dc)*, dc in next st, (2 dc, ch 2, 2 dc) in next corner ch-2 sp, dc in each st around, working (2 dc, ch 2, 2 dc) in each corner ch-2 sp; join with sl st to first dc (3rd ch of beg ch-3). Cut yarn. *(157 dc across short sides, 211 dc across long sides & 4 corner ch-2 sps)*

4. Front Layer:

Rnd 1: With right side facing, using smaller hook, join C1 with standing sc in any corner ch-2 sp *(before dc-sts)*, ch 2, sc in same sp *(after the dc-sts)*, working in BLO of sl sts, sc in each st around, working (sc, ch 2, sc) in each corner; join with sl st to first sc. Do NOT cut yarn. *(151 sc across short sides, 205 sc across long sides & 4 corner ch-2 sps)*

Rnds 2-4: (C1) Ch 1, sc in BLO of same st as joining, working in BLO *(except corners)*, sc in each st around, working (sc, ch 2, sc) in each corner ch-2 sp; join with sl st to first sc.

At the end of Round 4, cut yarn.

There are 157 sc across short sides, 211 sc across long sides & 4 corner ch-2 sps. (Every round has an increase of 2 stitches on each side.)

5. Join Front & Back Layers

Notes:

a. The entire round is worked through the BLO of both the Front Layer and the corresponding Back Layer stitches together.

b. Corners are worked through the corresponding ch-2 spaces on both layers.

Joining Round: With right side facing, using smaller hook, join C1 with standing sc in any corner ch-2 sp, 2 sc in same sp; working in BLO, sl st in each st around, working 3 sc in each corner ch-2 sp; join with sl st to first sc. Cut yarn and sew in all ends. *(157 sl sts across short sides, 211 sl sts across long sides & 4 corner 3-sc)*

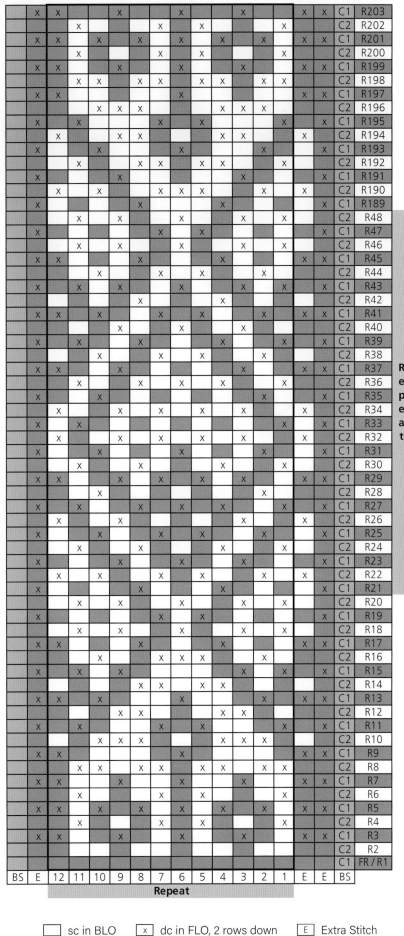

☐ sc in BLO   ☒ dc in FLO, 2 rows down   E Extra Stitch

■ Border Stitch (BS)   ■ C1   ☐ C2

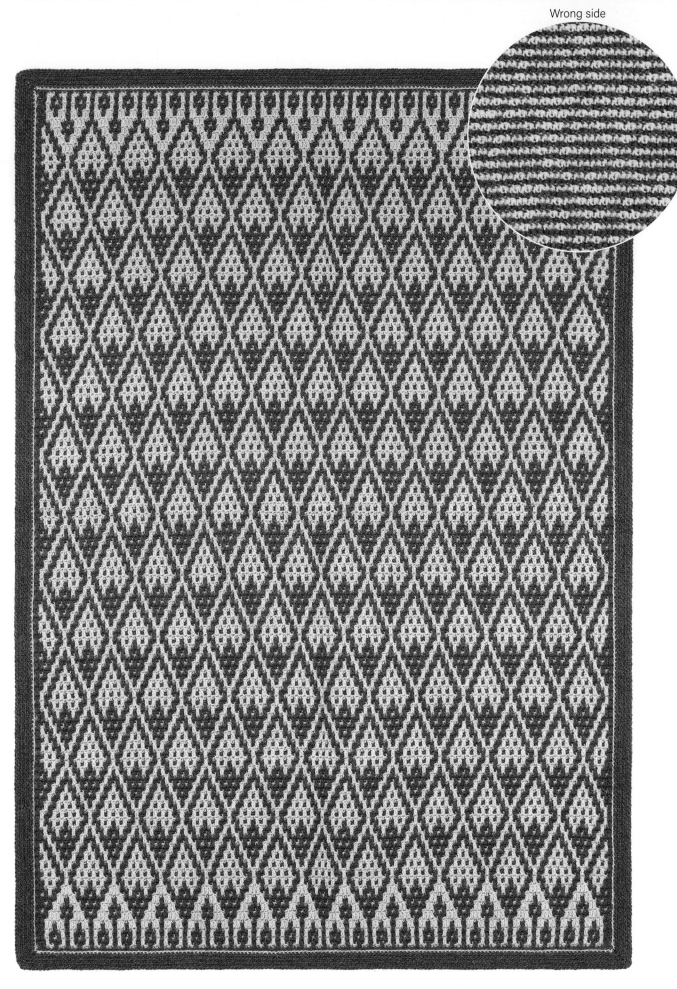

About 37" (93 cm) wide and 52" (132 cm) long

TILES

Materials

DK / Light Weight Yarn

Jody Long Alba (50% Merino Wool, 25% Alpaca, 25% Viscose)

1 ball - 3.52 oz (382 yards) / 100 g (350 m)

Color 1 (C1): Winter (#019) - 5 balls

Color 2 (C2): Loch (#003) - 4 balls

Color 3 (C3): Marmalade (#015) - 1 ball

Size G-6 (4.00 mm) Crochet Hook

Scissors and Tapestry Needle

Finished Size & Gauge

Blanket: About 37" (93 cm) wide and 48" (123 cm) long

Gauge: 20 stitches and 20 rows = 4" (10 cm) approximately.

Note: The finished size of the blanket might differ due to the gauge needed for the choice of yarn used. The overall size of the blanket can be customized by adding or removing pattern repeats, which will affect the amount of yarn required.

Multiple (Stitch Pattern Repeat): 24 + 5

There are 24 stitches in each pattern repeat.

The additional 5 stitches are the 2 Border Stitches plus 2 Extra Stitches at the beginning of a row and 1 Extra Stitch at the end of the row.

Pattern Notes

1 The Blanket pictured has 7 stitch pattern repeats.

2 Refer to General Pattern Notes.

3 See section on Special Stitches, if needed.

Skill Level

Intermediate or Adventurous Beginner

BLANKET

Foundation Row / Row 1: *(Right Side)* (C1) Make 173 FSC. Cut yarn. Do not turn your work. Continue with row 2. *(173 sc)*

Or for Chain Foundation:

Foundation Row / Row 1: *(Right Side)* (C1) Ch 174, starting in 2nd ch from hook, sc in each ch across. Cut yarn, leaving a tail. Do not turn your work. Continue with Row 2. *(173 sc)*

Row 2: (C2) BS, ch 1, 171 sc, ch 1, BS. *(173 sc)*

Row 3: (C1) BS, ch 1, 1 dc, 1 sc, [1 dc, 1 sc, 1 dc, 17 sc, (1 dc, 1 sc) 2 times] 7 times, 1 dc, ch 1, BS. *(143 sc & 30 dc) [20 sc & 4 dc]*

Repeat Begins:

Row 4: (C2) BS, ch 1, 2 sc, [1 sc, 1 dc, 19 sc, 1 dc, 2 sc] 7 times, 1 sc, ch 1, BS. *(159 sc & 14 dc) [21 sc & 2 dc]*

Row 5: (C1) BS, ch 1, 1 dc, 1 sc, [2 sc, 2 dc, 15 sc, 2 dc, 3 sc] 7 times, 1 dc, ch 1, BS. *(143 sc & 30 dc) [20 sc & 4 dc]*

Row 6: (C2) BS, ch 1, 2 sc, [4 sc, 1 dc, (6 sc, 1 dc) 2 times, 5 sc] 7 times, 1 sc, ch 1, BS. *(152 sc & 21 dc) [21 sc & 3 dc]*

Row 7: (C1) BS, ch 1, 1 dc, 1 sc, [2 dc, 1 sc, 1 dc, (1 sc, 1 dc, 4 sc, 1 dc) 2 times, 1 sc, 1 dc, 1 sc, 2 dc, 1 sc] 7 times, 1 dc, ch 1, BS. *(101 sc & 72 dc) [14 sc & 10 dc]*

Row 8: (C2) BS, ch 1, 1 sc, 1 dc, [4 sc, 1 dc, (1 sc, 1 dc, 2 sc, 1 dc, 1 sc, 1 dc) 2 times, 4 sc, 1 dc] 7 times, 1 sc, ch 1, BS. *(116 sc & 57 dc) [16 sc & 8 dc]*

Row 9: (C1) BS, ch 1, 1 dc, 1 sc, [1 dc, 4 sc, (1 sc, 1 dc, 2 sc, 1 dc, 1 sc) 2 times, 3 sc, 1 dc, 1 sc] 7 times, 1 dc, ch 1, BS. *(101 sc & 72 dc) [14 sc & 10 dc]*

Row 10: (C2) BS, ch 1, 1 sc, 1 dc, [1 sc, 1 dc, 4 sc, 1 dc, 2 sc, 1 dc, (1 sc, 1 dc) 2 times, 2 sc, 1 dc, 4 sc, 1 dc, 1 sc, 1 dc] 7 times, 1 sc, ch 1, BS. *(116 sc & 57 dc) [16 sc & 8 dc]*

Row 11: (C1) BS, ch 1, 1 dc, 1 sc, [1 dc, 1 sc, 1 dc, 4 sc, (1 dc, 2 sc, 1 dc, 1 sc) 2 times, 3 sc, (1 dc, 1 sc) 2 times] 7 times, 1 dc, ch 1, BS. *(115 sc & 58 dc) [16 sc & 8 dc]*

Row 12: (C2) BS, ch 1, 1 sc, 1 dc, [(1 sc, 1 dc) 2 times, 2 sc, 1 dc, (4 sc, 1 dc) 2 times, 2 sc, 1 dc, (1 sc, 1 dc) 2 times] 7 times, 1 sc, ch 1, BS. *(116 sc & 57 dc) [16 sc & 8 dc]*

Row 13: (C1) BS, ch 1, 1 dc, 1 sc [(1 dc, 1 sc) 2 times, (2 dc, 3 sc, 2 dc, 1 sc) 2 times, (1 dc, 1 sc) 2 times] 7 times, 1 dc, ch 1, BS. *(87 sc & 86 dc) [12 sc & 12 dc]*

Row 14: (C2) BS, ch 1, 1 sc, 1 dc, [(1 sc, 1 dc) 2 times, 4 sc, 1 dc, 5 sc, 1 dc, 4 sc, 1 dc, (1 sc, 1 dc) 2 times] 7 times, 1 sc, ch 1, BS. *(123 sc & 50 dc) [17 sc & 7 dc]*

Row 15: (C1) BS, ch 1, 1 dc, 1 sc, [1 dc, 1 sc, 1 dc, 3 sc, 2 dc, 7 sc, 2 dc, 3 sc, (1 dc, 1 sc) 2 times] 7 times, 1 dc, ch 1, BS. *(115 sc & 58 dc) [16 sc & 8 dc]*

Row 16: (C2) BS, ch 1, 1 sc, 1 dc, [1 sc, 1 dc, 7 sc, 1 dc, 3 sc, 1 dc, 7 sc, 1 dc, 1 sc, 1 dc] 7 times, 1 sc, ch 1, BS. *(137 sc & 36 dc) [19 sc & 5 dc]*

Row 17: (C1) BS, ch 1, 1 dc, 1 sc, [1 dc, 7 sc, 1 dc, (1 sc, 1 dc) 3 times, 7 sc, 1 dc, 1 sc] 7 times, 1 dc, ch 1, BS. *(129 sc & 44 dc) [18 sc & 6 dc]*

Row 18: (C2) BS, ch 1, 1 sc, 1 dc, [1 sc, 1 dc, 7 sc, 1 dc, 3 sc, 1 dc, 7 sc, 1 dc, 1 sc, 1 dc] 7 times, 1 sc, ch 1, BS. *(137 sc & 36 dc) [19 sc & 5 dc]*

Row 19: (C1) BS, ch 1, 1 dc, 1 sc, [1 dc, 1 sc, 1 dc, 3 sc, 2 dc, 7 sc, 2 dc, 3 sc, (1 dc, 1 sc) 2 times] 7 times, 1 dc, ch 1, BS. *(115 sc & 58 dc) [16 sc & 8 dc]*

Row 20: (C2) BS, ch 1, 1 sc, 1 dc, [(1 sc, 1 dc) 2 times, 4 sc, 1 dc, 5 sc, 1 dc, 4 sc, 1 dc, (1 sc, 1 dc) 2 times] 7 times, 1 sc, ch 1, BS. *(123 sc & 50 dc) [17 sc & 7 dc]*

Row 21: (C1) BS, ch 1, 1 dc, 1 sc, [(1 dc, 1 sc) 2 times, 2 dc, 3 sc, 2 dc, 1 sc, 2 dc, 3 sc, 2 dc, 1 sc, (1 dc, 1 sc) 2 times] 7 times, 1 dc, ch 1, BS. *(87 sc & 86 dc) [12 sc & 12 dc]*

Row 22: (C2) BS, ch 1, 1 sc, 1 dc, [(1 sc, 1 dc) 2 times, 2 sc, 1 dc, (4 sc, 1 dc) 2 times, 2 sc, 1 dc, (1 sc, 1 dc) 2 times] 7 times, 1 sc, ch 1, BS. *(116 sc & 57 dc) [16 sc & 8 dc]*

Row 23: (C1) BS, ch 1, 1 dc, 1 sc, [(1 dc, 1 sc) 2 times, 3 sc, (1 dc, 2 sc, 1 dc, 1 sc) 2 times, 3 sc, (1 dc, 1 sc) 2 times] 7 times, 1 dc, ch 1, BS. *(115 sc & 58 dc) [16 sc & 8 dc]*

Row 24: (C2) BS, ch 1, 1 sc, 1 dc, [1 sc, 1 dc, 4 sc, 1 dc, 2 sc, 1 dc, (1 sc, 1 dc) 2 times, 2 sc, 1 dc, 4 sc, 1 dc, 1 sc, 1 dc] 7 times, 1 sc, ch 1, BS. *(116 sc & 57 dc) [16 sc & 8 dc]*

Row 25: (C1) BS, ch 1, 1 dc, 1 sc, [1 dc, 4 sc, 1 dc, 1 sc, 2 dc, (1 sc, 1 dc) 2 times, 1 sc, 2 dc, 1 sc, 1 dc, 4 sc, 1 dc, 1 sc] 7 times, 1 dc, ch 1, BS. *(101 sc & 72 dc) [14 sc & 10 dc]*

Row 26: (C2) BS, ch 1, 1 sc, 1 dc, [4 sc, 1 dc, 1 sc, 1 dc, 2 sc, 1 dc, (1 sc, 1 dc) 2 times, 2 sc, 1 dc, 1 sc, 1 dc, 4 sc, 1 dc] 7 times, 1 sc, ch 1, BS. *(116 sc & 57 dc) [16 sc & 8 dc]*

Row 27: (C1) BS, ch 1, 1 dc, 1 sc, [2 dc, (1 sc, 1 dc) 2 times, (4 sc, 1 dc, 1 sc, 1 dc) 2 times, 1 sc, 2 dc, 1 sc] 7 times, 1 dc, ch 1, BS. *(101 sc & 72 dc) [14 sc & 10 dc]*

Row 28: (C2) BS, ch 1, 2 sc, [4 sc, 1 dc, (6 sc, 1 dc) 2 times, 5 sc] 7 times, 1 sc, ch 1, BS. *(152 sc & 21 dc) [21 sc & 3 dc]*

Row 29: (C1) BS, ch 1, 1 dc, 1 sc, [2 sc, 2 dc, 15 sc, 2 dc, 3 sc] 7 times, 1 dc, ch 1, BS. *(143 sc & 30 dc) [20 sc & 4 dc]*

Row 30: (C2) BS, ch 1, 2 sc, [1 sc, 1 dc, 19 sc, 1 dc, 2 sc] 7 times, 1 sc, ch 1, BS. *(159 sc & 14 dc) [22 sc & 2 dc]*

Row 31: (C1) BS, ch 1, 1 dc, 1 sc, [1 dc, 1 sc, 1 dc, 17 sc, (1 dc, 1 sc) 2 times] 7 times, 1 dc, ch 1, BS. *(143 sc & 30 dc) [20 sc & 4 dc]*

Rows 32-227: Repeat Rows 4-31 *(28 rows)* seven times more.

BORDER

Follow instructions for Making the Border.

1. Secure the Yarn Tails.

2. Special Round: With right side facing and C3, join with standing sl st in first st on Foundation Row/Row 1; sl st around, working ch 2 in corners; join with sl st to first ch-2 sp. Cut yarn. *(173 sl sts across top and bottom edges, 227 sl sts across right and left edges & 4 corner ch-2 sps)*

3. Back Layer:

Rnd 1: With wrong side facing and C3, join with standing dc in any corner ch-2 sp on bottom edge; (dc, ch 2, 2 dc) in same sp; dc in each st around *(taking care not to skip the sts before and after ch-2 corner sps)*, working (2 dc, ch 2, 2 dc) in each corner ch-2 sp; join with sl st to first *(standing)* dc. Do NOT cut yarn. *(177 dc across short sides, 231 dc across long sides & 4 corner ch-2 sps)*

Legend:

- ☐ sc in BLO
- ☒ X dc in FLO, 2 rows down
- ▨ Border Stitch (BS)
- E Extra Stitch
- ☐ C1
- ▨ C2

Chart rounds (right side column), bottom to top: FR/R1 (C1), R2 (C2), R3 (C1), R4 (C2), R5 (C1), R6 (C2), R7 (C1), R8 (C2), R9 (C1), R10 (C2), R11 (C1), R12 (C2), R13 (C1), R14 (C2), R15 (C1), R16 (C2), R17 (C1), R18 (C2), R19 (C1), R20 (C2), R21 (C1), R22 (C2), R23 (C1), R24 (C2), R25 (C1), R26 (C2), R27 (C1), R28 (C2), R29 (C1), R30 (C2), R31 (C1).

Column labels (bottom, left to right): BS | E | 24 | 23 | 22 | 21 | 20 | 19 | 18 | 17 | 16 | 15 | 14 | 13 | 12 | 11 | 10 | 9 | 8 | 7 | 6 | 5 | 4 | 3 | 2 | 1 | E | E | BS

Repeat

(Right margin: **Repeat**)

Rnd 2: (C3) Ch 3 *(counts as first dc)*, dc in next st, (2 dc, ch 2, 2 dc) in next corner ch-2 sp, dc in each st around, working (2 dc, ch 2, 2 dc) in each corner ch-2 sp; join with sl st to first dc (3rd *ch of beg ch-3)*. Cut yarn. *(181 dc across short sides, 235 dc across long sides & 4 corner ch-2 sps)*

4. Front Layer:

Rnd 1: With right side facing and C3, join with standing sc in any corner ch-2 sp *(before dc-sts)*, ch 2, sc in same sp *(after the dc-sts)*, working in BLO of sl sts, sc in each st around, working (sc, ch 2, sc) in each corner; join with sl st to first sc. Do NOT cut yarn.

(175 sc across short sides, 229 sc across long sides & 4 corner ch-2 sps)

Rnds 2-4: (C3) Ch 1, sc in BLO of same st as joining, working in BLO *(except corners)*, sc in each st around, working (sc, ch 2, sc) in each corner ch-2 sp; join with sl st to first sc.

At the end of Round 4, cut yarn.

There are 181 sc across short sides, 235 sc across long sides & 4 corner ch-2 sps. *(Every round has an increase of 2 stitches on each side.)*

5. Join Front & Back Layers

Notes:

a. The entire round is worked through the BLO of both the Front Layer and the corresponding Back Layer stitches together.

b. Corners are worked through the corresponding ch-2 spaces on both layers.

Joining Round: With right side facing and C2, join with standing sc in any corner ch-2 sp, 2 sc in same sp; working in BLO, sl st in each st around, working 3 sc in each corner ch-2 sp; join with sl st to first sc. Cut yarn and sew in all ends.

(181 sl sts across short sides, 235 sl sts across long sides & 4 corner 3-sc)

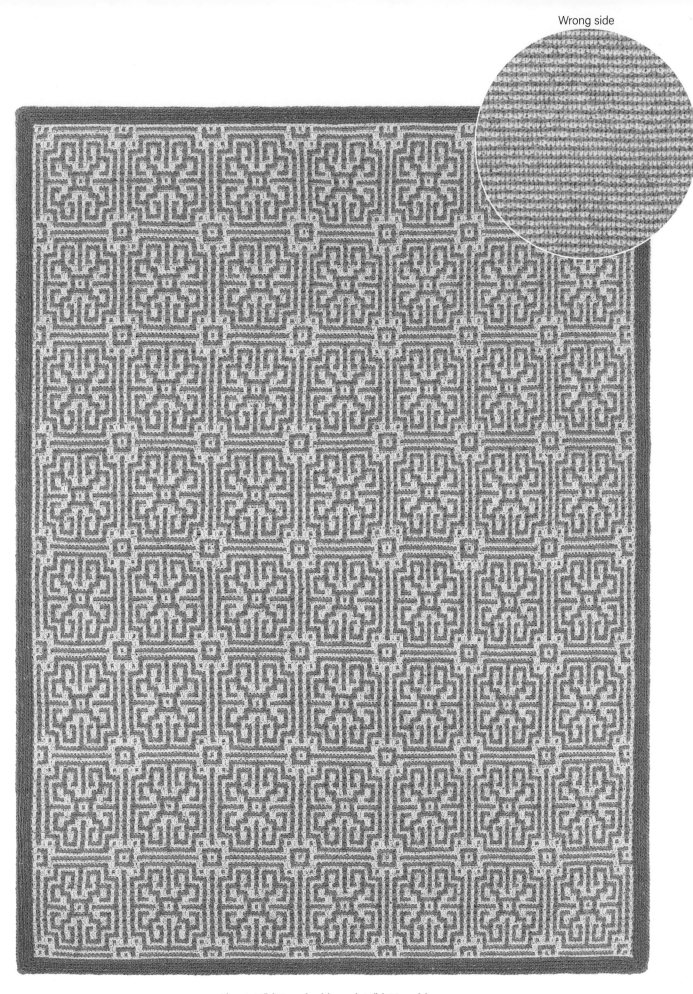

About 37" (93 cm) wide and 48" (123 cm) long

Tutti FRUTTI

Materials

Sport / Fine Weight Yarn

Queensland United (55% Lambswool, 45% Cotton)

1 ball – 1.76 oz (251 yards) / 50 g (230 m)

Main Color (MC): Ivory (#25) – 5 balls

Contrasting Colors (CC):

Color 1 (C1): Amber (#04) – 1 ball

Color 2 (C2): Lichen (#07) – 1 ball

Color 3 (C3): Passion Flower (#17) – 1 ball

Color 4 (C4): Aconite (#03) – 1 ball

Color 5 (C5): Rhubarb (#15) – 1 ball

Color 6 (C6): Kingfisher (#20) – 1 ball

Size E-4 (3.5 mm) crochet hook (Motifs and Border)

Size G-6 (4 mm) crochet hook (Joining Motifs)

3″ (8 cm) wide piece of Card (for Fringe)

Scissors and Tapestry Needle

Finished Size & Gauge

Blanket: About 38″ (96 cm) square

Gauge: Each Motif is about 6″ (15 cm) square.

Note: The finished size of the blanket might differ due to the gauge needed for the choice of yarn used. The overall size of the blanket can be customized by adding or removing pattern repeats, which will affect the amount of yarn required.

Pattern Notes:

1. The blanket pictured is 6 motifs wide and 6 motifs long.

2. The Motifs and Border of the Blanket use Overlay Mosaic technique, worked in rounds.

3. Refer to General Pattern Notes.

4. See section on Special Stitches, if needed.

Skill Level

Intermediate or Adventurous Beginner

MOTIF NOTES

1. Each Motif uses the Main Color and one Contrasting Color.

2. From Round 3, all single crochet stitches are worked in the back loop only (BLO), except for the corners. The double crochet stitches are worked in the front loop only (FLO) of the corresponding stitch two rounds below.

3. All rounds are worked with right side facing.

4. Do NOT fasten off at the end of each round (after making the ch-3 string).

5. The last single crochet before the third corner and the first single crochet of the third corner are worked over the ch-3 string from previous round.

CHART NOTES

1. Each Motif is worked in rounds, starting with a Magic Ring (MR).

2. Each block on the chart represents one stitch, except for the corner blocks (with ∞), which represent two chain stitches.

3. The corners in all the rounds are worked in the corner chain-2 spaces.

4. Each round is worked in one color only. From Round 3, colors are alternated every round.

5. Round 1 ends with a slip stitch in the first sc.

6. From Round 2 onwards, the rounds end with a slip stitch in the first single crochet, and then 3 chain stitches are made and the hook is removed.

7. Round 2 starts with one chain stitch, and the first corner (sc, ch 2, sc) is worked in the ch-2 space of Round 1.

8. The starting point of each round is opposite to the ending point of the previous round.

9. Round 3 (MC) starts with a standing single crochet in the chain-2 space diagonally opposite the end of Round 2.

10. The last single crochet before the third corner and the first single crochet of the third corner are worked over the ch-3 string from previous round.

BLANKET

Motif (Make 36 – 6 motifs using MC & one CC)

Rnd 1: *(Right Side)* Using CC and smaller hook, make a magic ring; ch 1, [sc in ring, ch 2] 4 times; join with sl st to first sc. *(4 sc & 4 corner ch-2 sps)*

Rnd 2: Ch 1, [(sc, ch 2, sc) in next ch-2 sp, sc in next st] 4 times; join with sl st to first sc. Ch 3 and remove hook.
(3 sc on each side, 4 corner ch-2 sps & 1 ch-3 string)

Rnd 3: *(see Motif Notes)* Join MC with standing sc in corner ch-2 sp opposite the ch-3 string, ch 2, sc in same sp *(first corner made)*, sc in each of next 3 sc, (sc, ch 2, sc) in next corner ch-2 sp *(second corner made)*, sc in each of next 2 sc; working over ch-3 string, sc in next sc *(image 1)*, sc in next corner ch-2 sp, ch 2; *(not working over string)* sc in same sp *(third corner made)* *(image 2)*, sc in each of next 3 sc, (sc, ch 2, sc) in next corner ch-2 sp *(fourth corner made)*, sc in each of next 3 sc; join with sl st to first sc. Ch 3 and remove hook. *(image 3)* *(5 sc on each side, 4 corner ch-2 sps & 1 ch-3 string)*

Rnd 4: Insert hook in CC loop *(from Rnd 2)*, [(sc, ch 2, sc) in corner ch-2 sp, 5 sc] 4 times; join with sl st to first sc. Ch 3 and remove hook. *(images 4 & 5)*

Remember to work over ch-3 string with last sc before 3rd corner and first sc of corner. (7 sc on each side, 4 corner ch-2 sps & 1 ch-3 string)

Note: *Remember to work over the chain-3 string at the third corner on every round!*

Rnd 5: Insert hook in MC loop *(from Rnd 3)*, [(sc, ch 2, sc) in corner ch-2 sp, 3 sc, 1 dc, 3 sc] 4 times; join with sl st to first sc. Ch 3 and remove hook. *(image 6)* *(8 sc & 1 dc on each side, 4 corner ch-2 sps & 1 ch-3 string)*

Rnd 6: Insert hook in CC loop, [(sc, ch 2, sc) in corner ch-2 sp, 3 sc, 1 dc, 1 sc, 1 dc, 3 sc] 4 times; join with sl st to first sc. Ch 3 and remove hook. *(9 sc & 2 dc on each side, 4 corner ch-2 sps & 1 ch-3 string)*

Rnd 7: Insert hook in MC loop, [(sc, ch 2, sc) in corner ch-2 sp, 5 sc, 1 dc, 5 sc] 4 times; join with sl st to first sc. Ch 3 and remove hook. *(12 sc & 1 dc on each side, 4 corner ch-2 sps & 1 ch-3 string)*

Rnd 8: Insert hook in CC loop, [(sc, ch 2, sc) in corner ch-2 sp, 13 sc] 4 times; join with sl st to first sc. Ch 3 and remove hook. *(15 sc on each side, 4 corner ch-2 sps & 1 ch-3 string)*

Rnd 9: Insert hook in MC loop, [(sc, ch 2, sc) in corner ch-2 sp, 15 sc] 4 times; join with sl st to first sc. Ch 3 and remove hook. *(17 sc on each side, 4 corner ch-2 sps & 1 ch-3 string)*

Rnd 10: Insert hook in CC loop, [(sc, ch 2, sc) in corner ch-2 sp, 17 sc] 4 times; join with sl st to first sc. Ch 3 and remove hook. *(19 sc on each side, 4 corner ch-2 sps & 1 ch-3 string)*

Rnd 11: Insert hook in MC loop, [(sc, ch 2, sc) in corner ch-2 sp, 5 sc, 1 dc, (3 sc, 1 dc) 2 times, 5 sc] 4 times; join with sl st to first sc. Ch 3 and remove hook. *(18 sc & 3 dc on each side, 4 corner ch-2 sps & 1 ch-3 string)*

Rnd 12: Insert hook in CC loop, [(sc, ch 2, sc) in corner ch-2 sp, 3 sc, 1 dc, 3 sc, (1 dc, 1 sc) 3 times, (1 dc, 3 sc) 2 times] 4 times; join with sl st to first sc. Ch 3 and remove hook.
(17 sc & 6 dc on each side, 4 corner ch-2 sps & 1 ch-3 string)

Rnd 13: Insert hook in MC loop, [(sc, ch 2, sc) in corner ch-2 sp, (3 sc, 1 dc, 1 sc, 1 dc) 2 times, 1 sc, 1 dc, 3 sc, 1 dc, 1 sc, 1 dc, 3 sc] 4 times; join with sl st to first sc. Ch 3 and remove hook. *(18 sc & 7 dc on each side, 4 corner ch-2 sps & 1 ch-3 string)*

Rnd 14: Insert hook in CC loop, [(sc, ch 2, sc) in corner ch-2 sp, 3 sc, (1 dc, 1 sc) 2 times, (1 dc, 3 sc, 1 dc, 1 sc) 2 times, 1 dc, 1 sc, 1 dc, 3 sc] 4 times; join with sl st to first sc. Ch 3 and remove hook.

(19 sc & 8 dc on each side, 4 corner ch-2 sps & 1 ch-3 string)

Rnd 15: Insert hook in MC loop, [(sc, ch 2, sc) in corner ch-2 sp, 5 sc, 1 dc, 1 sc, (1 dc, 5 sc) 2 times, 1 dc, 1 sc, 1 dc, 5 sc] 4 times; join with sl st to first sc. Ch 3 and remove hook.
(24 sc & 5 dc on each side, 4 corner ch-2 sps & 1 ch-3 string)

Rnd 16: Insert hook in CC loop, [(sc, ch 2, sc) in corner ch-2 sp, 29 sc] 4 times; join with sl st to first sc. Cut CC yarn.
(31 sc on each side, 4 corner ch-2 sps)

Rnd 17: Insert hook in MC loop, [(sc, ch 2, sc) in corner ch-2 sp, 31 sc] 4 times; join with sl st to first sc. Cut MC yarn. *(image 7)*
(33 sc on each side, 4 corner ch-2 sps)

Image 1

Image 2

Image 3

Image 4

Image 5

Image 6

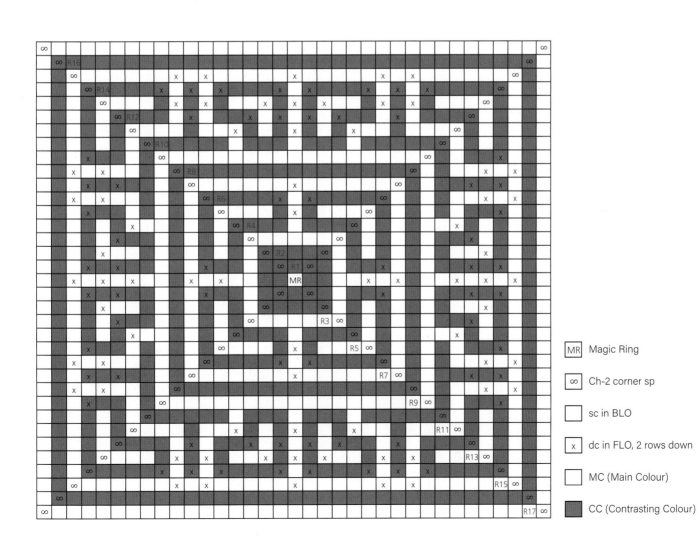

	MR	Magic Ring
	∞	Ch-2 corner sp
		sc in BLO
	x	dc in FLO, 2 rows down
		MC (Main Colour)
		CC (Contrasting Colour)

JOINING MOTIFS

When all the Motifs are made, use the Color Distribution Chart to lay out the Motifs (with right sides facing) – 6 motifs wide by 6 motifs long.

The motifs are crocheted together through both loops of the stitches on the last round. Following the Color Distribution Chart, first join the motifs together horizontally, and then join them vertically.

Color Distribution Chart

C2	C3	C4	C6	C5	C1
C5	C6	C2	C1	C4	C3
C4	C1	C5	C3	C2	C6
C3	C2	C6	C4	C1	C5
C1	C5	C3	C2	C6	C4
C6	C4	C1	C5	C3	C2

Joining Row: Holding first two motifs with wrong sides facing outwards (right sides together), using larger hook, working through both thicknesses, join MC with standing sc in any corner ch-2 sp, *[ch 1, skip next st, sc in next st] 16 times *(image 8)*, ch 1, skip next st, sc in next corner ch-2 sp**, ch 1 *(connection between motifs)*; holding next two motifs with wrong sides facing outwards, sc in corner ch-2 sp* *(image 9)*; repeat from * to * 5 times more, ending at ** on final repeat. Fasten off and weave in all ends.

Open the joined motifs with right side facing, making sure the ch-1 connections are not twisted, following the Color Distribution Chart, place the next new motif (wrong side facing - right sides together) on top of a joined motif, and repeat the Joining Row. Repeat this until all motifs are joined horizontally.

Then repeat the procedure and use the Joining Row to connect all the motifs vertically. The connecting ch-1 stitches go over the horizontal connecting ch-1 stitches. *(image 10)*

BORDER

***Note:** All rounds of the Border are worked with right side facing.*

Rnd 1: With right side facing, join CC1 with standing sc in any corner ch-2 sp, (ch 2, sc) in same sp *(first corner made)*;

Side

*[ch 1, skip next st, sc in next st] 16 times, ch 1, skip next st**, hdc in next ch-2 sp, ch 1, skip joining st, hdc in next ch-2 sp*; repeat from * to * 5 times more, ending at ** on final repeat;

Corner

(sc, ch 2, sc) in next corner ch-2 sp.

Repeat Side & Corner 2 times more, and then repeat Side once more; join with sl st to first sc. Cut yarn and sew in ends. *(98 sc, 10 hdc & 107 ch-1 sps across each side & 4 corner ch-2 sps)*

Rnd 2: Join CC2 with standing sc in any corner ch-2 sp, (ch 2, sc) in same corner ch-2 sp *(first corner made)*, *ch 1, [sc in next ch-1 sp, ch 1, skip next st] across to next corner**, (sc, ch 2, sc) in next corner ch-2 sp*; repeat from * to *, ending at ** on final repeat; join with sl st to first sc. Cut yarn and sew in ends. *(109 sc & 108 ch-1 sps across each side & 4 corner ch-2 sps)*

Rnd 3: With CC3, repeat Rnd 2. *(110 sc & 109 ch-1 sps across each side & 4 corner ch-2 sps)*

Rnd 4: With CC4, repeat Rnd 2. *(111 sc & 110 ch-1 sps across each side & 4 corner ch-2 sps)*

Rnd 5: With CC5, repeat Rnd 2. *(112 sc & 111 ch-1 sps across each side & 4 corner ch-2 sps)*

Rnd 6: With CC6, repeat Rnd 2. *(113 sc & 112 ch-1 sps across each side & 4 corner ch-2 sps)*

Rnd 7: Join MC with standing sc in any corner ch-2 sp, (ch 2, sc) in same corner *(first corner made)*, *sc in next st, [sc in next sp, sc in next st] across to next corner**, (sc, ch 2, sc) in corner ch-2 sp*; repeat from * to *, ending at ** on final repeat; join with sl st to first sc. Cut yarn and sew in ends. *(227 sc across each side & 4 corner ch-2 sps) (images 11 & 12)*

FINAL TOUCH

Fringe (Make 4) *Refer to Making A Tassel.*

A fringe is attached to each corner and at intervals along the sides.

Preparation:

1. Cut a piece of Card 3" wide.

2. Cut 24 lengths of MC, 60" long. (One 60" length for each Fringe.)

Method:

Follow steps 1 to 5 of Making a Fringe for each fringe placement.

Attach a Fringe to each corner chain-2 space.

Attach a Fringe to the single crochet stitches (on the last round) which are aligned with the chain-1 spaces between the half-double crochets (on Round 1).

Image 7

Image 8

Image 9

Image 10

Image 11

Image 12

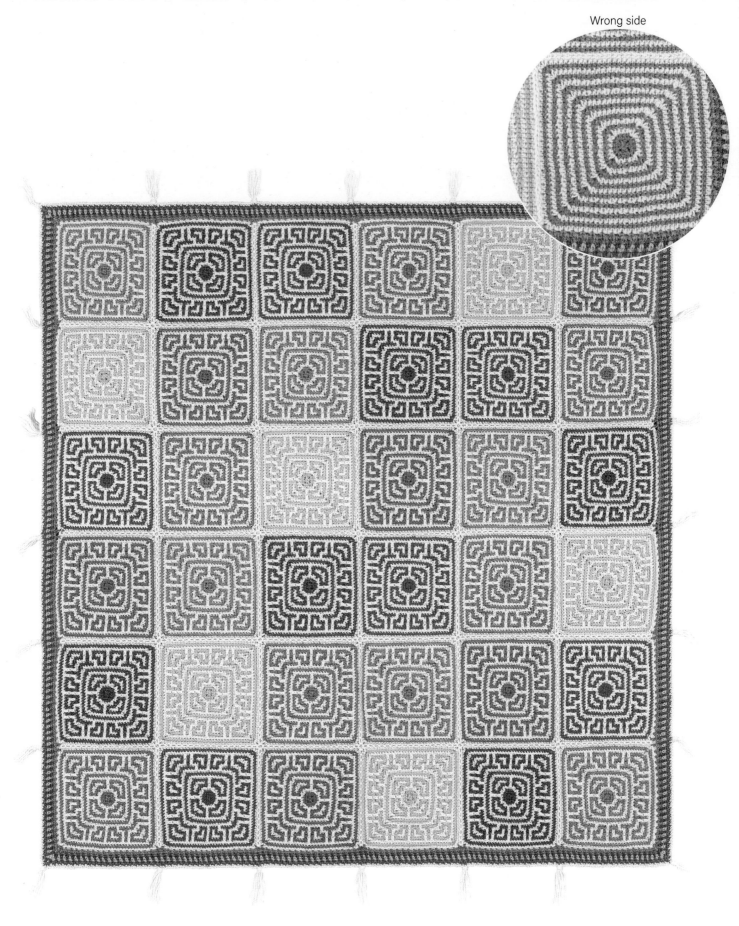

About 38″ (96 cm) square

Between WAVES

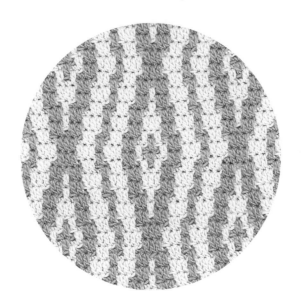

Materials

Worsted / Medium Weight Yarn

Juniper Moon Farm Moonshine (40% Alpaca, 40% Wool, 20% Organic Silk)

1 ball – 3.52 oz (197 yards)/ 100 g (180 m)

Color 1 (C1): Moonbeam (#02) – 6 skeins

Color 2 (C2): Honeycomb (#67) – 7 skeins

Size I-9 (5.5 mm) crochet hook (Blanket body and Special Round of the Border)

Size H-8 (5 mm) crochet hook (Front and Back Layers of the Border)

4" (10 cm) wide piece of Card (for Tassels)

Scissors and Tapestry Needle

Finished Size & Gauge

Blanket: About 34" (85 cm) wide and 47" (118 cm) long

Gauge: 16 stitches and 16 rows = 4" (10 cm) approximately.

Note: The finished size of the blanket might differ due to the gauge needed for the choice of yarn used. The overall size of the blanket can be customized by adding or removing pattern repeats, which will affect the amount of yarn required.

Multiple (Stitch Pattern Repeat): 26 + 21

There are 26 stitches in each pattern repeat.

The additional 21 stitches are the 2 Border Stitches plus 1 Extra Stitch at the beginning of a row and 18 Extra Stitches at the end of the row.

Pattern Notes

1 The Blanket pictured has 4 stitch pattern repeats.

2 Refer to General Pattern Notes.

3 See section on Special Stitches, if needed.

Skill Level

Intermediate or Adventurous Beginner

BLANKET

Foundation Row / Row 1: *(Right Side)* (C1) Using larger hook, make 125 FSC. Cut yarn. Do not turn your work. Continue with row 2. *(125 sc)*

Or for Chain Foundation:

Foundation Row / Row 1: *(Right Side)* (C1) Using larger hook, ch 126, starting in 2nd ch from hook, sc in each ch across. Cut yarn, leaving a tail. Do not turn your work. Continue with Row 2. *(125 sc)*

Row 2: (C2) BS, ch 1, 123 sc, ch 1, BS. *(125 sc)*

Repeat Begins:

Row 3: (C1) BS, ch 1, 1 dc, [3 dc, 1 sc, 3 dc, 3 sc, 3 dc, 1 sc, 3 dc, 2 sc, 1 dc, 3 sc, 1 dc, 2 sc] 4 times, 3 dc, 1 sc, 3 dc, 3 sc, 3 dc, 1 sc, 4 dc, ch 1, BS. (55 sc & 70 dc) [12 sc & 14 dc]

Row 4: (C2) BS, ch 1, 1 sc, [3 sc, 1 dc, 3 sc, 3 dc, 3 sc, 1 dc, 3 sc, 2 dc, 2 sc, 1 dc, 2 sc, 2 dc] 4 times, 3 sc, 1 dc, 3 sc, 3 dc, 3 sc, 1 dc, 4 sc, ch 1, BS. (80 sc & 45 dc) [16 sc & 10 dc]

Row 5: (C1) BS, ch 1, 1 dc, [2 dc, 2 sc, 2 dc, 5 sc, 2 dc, 2 sc, 2 dc, 3 sc, 1 dc, 1 sc, 1 dc, 3 sc] 4 times, 2 dc, 2 sc, 2 dc, 5 sc, 2 dc, 2 sc, 3 dc, ch 1, BS. (75 sc & 50 dc) [16 sc & 10 dc]

Row 6: (C2) BS, ch 1, 1 sc, [2 sc, 1 dc, 3 sc, 2 dc, 1 sc, 2 dc, 3 sc, 1 dc, (3 sc, 2 dc) 2 times, 1 sc] 4 times, 2 sc, 1 dc, 3 sc, 2 dc, 1 sc, 2 dc, 3 sc, 1 dc, 3 sc, ch 1, BS. (79 sc & 46 dc) [16 sc & 10 dc]

Row 7: (C1) BS, ch 1, 1 dc, [(2 dc, 1 sc, 3 dc, 2 sc, 1 dc, 2 sc, 3 dc, 1 sc, (3 dc, 2 sc) 2 times, 1 dc] 4 times, 2 dc, 1 sc, 3 dc, 2 sc, 1 dc, 2 sc, 3 dc, 1 sc, 3 dc, ch 1, BS. (48 sc & 77 dc) [10 sc & 16 dc]

Row 8: (C2) BS, ch 1, 1 sc, [2 sc, 1 dc, 3 sc, 2 dc, 1 sc, 2 dc, 3 sc, 1 dc, (3 sc, 2 dc) 2 times, 1 sc] 4 times, 2 sc, 1 dc, 3 sc, 2 dc, 1 sc, 2 dc, 3 sc, 1 dc, 3 sc, ch 1, BS. (79 sc & 46 dc) [16 sc & 10 dc]

Row 9: (C1) BS, ch 1, 1 dc, [1 dc, 2 sc, 2 dc, 3 sc, 1 dc, 3 sc, 2 dc, 2 sc, 2 dc, (3 sc, 1 dc) 2 times] 4 times, 1 dc, 2 sc, 2 dc, 3 sc, 1 dc, 3 sc, 2 dc, 2 sc, 2 dc, ch 1, BS. (76 sc & 49 dc) [16 sc & 10 dc]

Row 10: (C2) BS, ch 1, 1 sc, [1 sc, 1 dc, (3 sc, 2 dc) 2 times, 3 sc, 1 dc, 3 sc, 2 dc, 1 sc, 2 dc, 2 sc] 4 times, 1 sc, 1 dc, (3 sc, 2 dc) 2 times, 3 sc, 1 dc, 2 sc, ch 1, BS. (79 sc & 46 dc) [16 sc & 10 dc]

Row 11: (C1) BS, ch 1, 1 dc, [1 dc, 1 sc, (3 dc, 2 sc) 2 times, 3 dc, 1 sc, 3 dc, 2 sc, 1 dc, 2 sc, 2 dc] 4 times, 1 dc, 1 sc, (3 dc, 2 sc) 2 times, 3 dc, 1 sc, 2 dc, ch 1, BS. (48 sc & 77 dc) [10 sc & 16 dc]

Row 12: (C2) BS, ch 1, 1 sc, [1 sc, 1 dc, (3 sc, 2 dc) 2 times, 3 sc, 1 dc, 3 sc, 2 dc, 1 sc, 2 dc, 2 sc] 4 times, 1 sc, 1 dc, (3 sc, 2 dc) 2 times, 3 sc, 1 dc, 2 sc, ch 1, BS. (79 sc & 46 dc) [16 sc & 10 dc]

Row 13: (C1) BS, ch 1, 1 dc, [2 sc, 2 dc, 3 sc, 1 dc, 1 sc, 1 dc, 3 sc, 2 dc, 2 sc, 2 dc, 5 sc, 2 dc] 4 times, 2 sc, 2 dc, 3 sc, 1 dc, 1 sc, 1 dc, 3 sc, 2 dc, 2 sc, 1 dc, ch 1, BS. (77 sc & 48 dc) [16 sc & 10 dc]

Row 14: (C2) BS, ch 1, 1 sc, [1 dc, 3 sc, 2 dc, 2 sc, 1 dc, 2 sc, 2 dc, 3 sc, 1 dc, 3 sc, 3 dc, 3 sc] 4 times, 1 dc, 3 sc, 2 dc, 2 sc, 1 dc, 2 sc, 2 dc, 3 sc, 1 sc, ch 1, BS. (78 sc & 47 dc) [16 sc & 10 dc]

Row 15: (C1) BS, ch 1, 1 dc, [1 sc, 3 dc, 2 sc, 1 dc, 3 sc, 1 dc, 2 sc, 3 dc, 1 sc, 3 dc, 3 sc, 3 dc] 4 times, 1 sc, 3 dc, 2 sc, 1 dc, 3 sc, 1 dc, 2 sc, 3 dc, 1 dc, ch 1, BS. (59 sc & 66 dc) [12 sc & 14 dc]

Row 16: (C2) BS, ch 1, 1 sc, [1 dc, 3 sc, 2 dc, 2 sc, 1 dc, 2 sc, 2 dc, 3 sc, 1 dc, 3 sc, 3 dc, 3 sc] 4 times, 1 dc, 3 sc, 2 dc, 2 sc, 1 dc, 2 sc, 2 dc, 3 sc, 1 sc, ch 1, BS. (78 sc & 47 dc) [16 sc & 10 dc]

Row 17: (C1) BS, ch 1, 1 dc, [2 sc, 2 dc, 3 sc, 1 dc, 1 sc, 1 dc, 3 sc, 2 dc, 2 sc, 2 dc, 5 sc, 2 dc] 4 times, 2 sc, 2 dc, 3 sc, 1 dc, 1 sc, 1 dc, 3 sc, 2 dc, 2 sc, 1 dc, ch 1, BS. (77 sc & 48 dc) [16 sc & 10 dc]

Row 18: (C2) BS, ch 1, 1 sc, [1 sc, 1 dc, (3 sc, 2 dc) 2 times, 3 sc, 1 dc, 3 sc, 2 dc, 1 sc, 2 dc, 2 sc] 4 times, 1 sc, 1 dc, (3 sc, 2 dc) 2 times, 3 sc, 1 dc, 2 sc, ch 1, BS. (79 sc & 46 dc) [16 sc & 10 dc]

Row 19: (C1) BS, ch 1, 1 dc, [1 dc, 1 sc, (3 dc, 2 sc) 2 times, 3 dc, 1 sc, 3 dc, 2 sc, 1 dc, 2 sc, 2 dc] 4 times, 1 dc, 1 sc, (3 dc, 2 sc) 2 times, 3 dc, 1 sc, 2 dc, ch 1, BS. (48 sc & 77 dc) [10 sc & 16 dc]

Row 20: (C2) BS, ch 1, 1 sc, [1 sc, 1 dc, (3 sc, 2 dc) 2 times, 3 sc, 1 dc, 3 sc, 2 dc, 1 sc, 2 dc, 2 sc] 4 times, 1 sc, 1 dc, (3 sc, 2 dc) 2 times, 3 sc, 1 dc, 2 sc, ch 1, BS. (79 sc & 46 dc) [16 sc & 10 dc]

Row 21: (C1) BS, ch 1, 1 dc, [1 dc, 2 sc, 2 dc, 3 sc, 1 dc, 3 sc, 2 dc, 2 sc, 2 dc, (3 sc, 1 dc) 2 times] 4 times, 1 dc, 2 sc, 2 dc, 3 sc, 1 dc, 3 sc, 2 dc, 2 sc, 2 dc, ch 1, BS. (76 sc & 49 dc) [16 sc & 10 dc]

Row 22: (C2) BS, ch 1, 1 sc, [2 sc, 1 dc, 3 sc, 2 dc, 1 sc, 2 dc, 3 sc, 1 dc, (3 sc, 2 dc) 2 times, 1 sc] 4 times, 2 sc, 1 dc, 3 sc, 2 dc, 1 sc, 2 dc, 3 sc, 1 dc, 3 sc, ch 1, BS. (79 sc & 46 dc) [16 sc & 10 dc]

Row 23: (C1) BS, ch 1, 1 dc, [2 dc, 1 sc, 3 dc, 2 sc, 1 dc, 2 sc, 3 dc, 1 sc, (3 dc, 2 sc) 2 times, 1 dc] 4 times, 2 dc, 1 sc, 3 dc, 2 sc, 1 dc, 2 sc, 3 dc, 1 sc, 3 dc, ch 1, BS. (48 sc & 77 dc) [10 sc & 16 dc]

Row 24: (C2) BS, ch 1, 1 sc, [2 sc, 1 dc, 3 sc, 2 dc, 1 sc, 2 dc, 3 sc, 1 dc, (3 sc, 2 dc) 2 times, 1 sc] 4 times, 2 sc, 1 dc, 3 sc, 2 dc, 1 sc, 2 dc, 3 sc, 1 dc, 3 sc, ch 1, BS. (79 sc & 46 dc) [16 sc & 10 dc]

Row 25: (C1) BS, ch 1, 1 dc, [2 dc, 2 sc, 2 dc, 5 sc, 2 dc, 2 sc, 2 dc, 3 sc, 1 dc, 1 sc, 1 dc, 3 sc] 4 times, 2 dc, 2 sc, 2 dc, 5 sc, 2 dc, 2 sc, 3 dc, ch 1, BS. (75 sc & 50 dc) [16 sc & 10 dc]

Row 26: (C2) BS, ch 1, 1 sc, [3 sc, 1 dc, 3 sc, 3 dc, 3 sc, 1 dc, 3 sc, 2 dc, 2 sc, 1 dc, 2 sc, 2 dc] 4 times, 3 sc, 1 dc, 3 sc, 3 dc, 3 sc, 1 dc, 4 sc, ch 1, BS. (80 sc & 45 dc) [16 sc & 10 dc]

Rows 27-170: Repeat Rows 3-26 *(24 rows)* six times more.

Row 171: Repeat Row 3.

BORDER

Follow instructions for Making the Border.

1. Secure the Yarn Tails.

2. Special Round: With right side facing, using larger hook, join C2 with standing sl st in first st on Foundation Row/Row 1; sl st around, working ch 2 in corners; join with sl st to first ch-2 sp. Cut yarn. *(125 sl sts across top and bottom edges, 171 sl sts across right and left edges & 4 corner ch-2 sps)*

3. Back Layer:

Rnd 1: With wrong side facing, using smaller hook, join C2 with standing dc in any corner ch-2 sp on bottom edge; (dc, ch 2, 2 dc) in same sp; dc in each st around *(taking care not to skip the sts before and after ch-2 corner sps)*, working (2 dc, ch 2, 2 dc) in each corner ch-2 sp; join with sl st to first *(standing)* dc. Do NOT cut yarn. *(129 dc across short sides, 175 dc across long sides & 4 corner ch-2 sps)*

Rnd 2: (C3) Ch 3 *(counts as first dc)*, dc in next st, (2 dc, ch 2, 2 dc) in next corner ch-2 sp, dc in each st around, working (2 dc, ch 2, 2 dc) in each corner ch-2 sp; join with sl st to first dc *(3rd ch of beg ch-3)*. Cut yarn. *(133 dc across short sides, 179 dc across long sides & 4 corner ch-2 sps)*

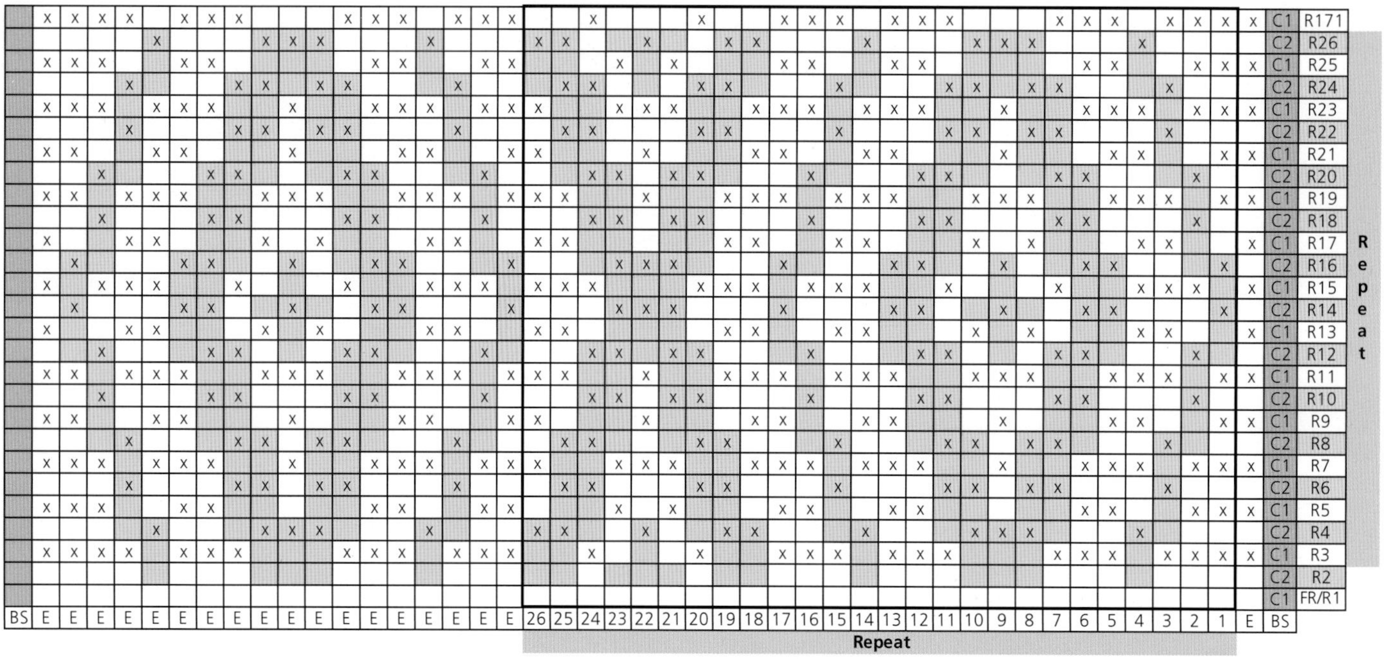

sc in BLO | x dc in FLO, 2 rows down | Border Stitch (BS) | E Extra Stitch | C1 | C2

4. Front Layer:

Rnd 1: With right side facing, using smaller hook, join C2 with standing sc in any corner ch-2 sp *(before dc-sts)*, ch 2, sc in same sp *(after the dc-sts)*, working in BLO of sl sts, sc in each st around, working (sc, ch 2, sc) in each corner; join with sl st to first sc. Do NOT cut yarn. *(127 sc across short sides, 173 sc across long sides & 4 corner ch-2 sps)*

Rnds 2-4: (C2) Ch 1, sc in BLO of same st as joining, working in BLO *(except corners)*, sc in each st around, working (sc, ch 2, sc) in each corner ch-2 sp; join with sl st to first sc.

At the end of Round 4, cut yarn.

There are 133 sc across short sides, 179 sc across long sides & 4 corner ch-2 sps. (Every round has an increase of 2 stitches on each side.)

5. Join Front & Back Layers

Notes:

a. *The entire round is worked through the BLO of both the Front Layer and the corresponding Back Layer stitches together.*

b. *Corners are worked through the corresponding ch-2 spaces on both layers.*

Joining Round: With right side facing, using smaller hook, join C2 with standing sc in any corner ch-2 sp, 2 sc in same sp; working in BLO, sl st in each st around, working 3 sc in each corner ch-2 sp; join with sl st to first sc. Cut yarn and sew in all ends. *(133 sl sts across short sides, 179 sl sts across long sides & 4 corner 3-sc)*

FINAL TOUCH

A tassel is attached to each corner of the Blanket.

Tassel (Make 4) *Refer to Making A Tassel.*

Preparation:

1. Cut a piece of card 4" (10 cm) wide

2. Long lengths (4 strands):

Cut two 30" (75 cm) strands of each color yarn (2 x Color 1 & 2 x Color 2).

3. Short Lengths (2 strands):

Cut two 20" (50 cm) strands of Color 2.

Method:

Follow steps 1 to 8 of Making a Tassel Method, wrapping the yarn three times around the card in step 1.

Repeat for each Tassel.

Wrong side

About 34″ (85 cm) wide and 47″ (118 cm) long

Rolling
DIAMONDS

Materials

DK / Light Weight Yarn

Jody Long Alba (50% Merino Wool, 25% Alpaca, 25% Viscose)

1 ball – 3.52 oz (382 yards) / 100 g (350 m)

Color 1 (C1): Marmalade (#015) - 5 balls

Color 2 (C2): Oats (#001) - 5 balls

Size G-6 (4.00 mm) Crochet Hook

Scissors and Tapestry Needle

Finished Size & Gauge

Blanket: About 35" (90 cm) wide and 49" (125 cm) long

Gauge: 20 stitches and 20 rows = 4" (10 cm) approximately.

Note: The finished size of the blanket might differ due to the gauge needed for the choice of yarn used. The overall size of the blanket can be customized by adding or removing pattern repeats, which will affect the amount of yarn required.

Multiple (Stitch Pattern Repeat): 20 + 3

There are 20 stitches in each pattern repeat.

The additional 3 stitches are the 2 Border Stitches plus 1 Extra Stitch at the beginning of a row.

Pattern Notes

The Blanket pictured has 8 stitch pattern repeats.

Refer to General Pattern Notes.

See section on Special Stitches, if needed.

Skill Level
Intermediate or Adventurous Beginner

BLANKET

Foundation Row / Row 1: *(Right Side)* (C1) Make 163 FSC. Cut yarn. Do not turn your work. Continue with row 2.

(163 sc)

Or for Chain Foundation:

Foundation Row / Row 1: *(Right Side)* (C1) Ch 164, starting in 2nd ch from hook, sc in each ch across. Cut yarn, leaving a tail. Do not turn your work. Continue with Row 2.

(163 sc)

Row 2: (C2) BS, ch 1, 161 sc, ch 1, BS. *(163 sc)*

Row 3: (C1) BS, ch 1, 1 sc, [1 sc, 1 dc, 2 sc, (3 dc, 2 sc, 1 dc, 2 sc) 2 times] 8 times, ch 1, BS. *(91 sc & 72 dc) [11 sc & 9 dc]*

Row 4: (C2) BS, ch 1, 1 dc, [2 sc, 1 dc, 4 sc, 2 dc, 1 sc, 2 dc, 4 sc, 1 dc, 2 sc, 1 dc] 8 times, ch 1, BS. *(106 sc & 57 dc) [13 sc & 7 dc]*

Row 5: (C1) BS, ch 1, 1 sc, [1 dc, 2 sc, 2 dc, 4 sc, 1 dc, 4 sc, 2 dc, 2 sc, 1 dc, 1 sc] 8 times, ch 1, BS. *(107 sc & 56 dc) [13 sc & 7 dc]*

Row 6: (C2) BS, ch 1, 1 sc, [1 sc, 1 dc, 3 sc, 2 dc, 5 sc, 2 dc, 3 sc, 1 dc, 2 sc] 8 times, ch 1, BS. *(115 sc & 48 dc) [14 sc & 6 dc]*

Row 7: (C1) BS, ch 1, 1 dc, [2 sc, 2 dc, 3 sc, 2 dc, 1 sc, 2 dc, 3 sc, 2 dc, 2 sc, 1 dc] 8 times, ch 1, BS. *(90 sc & 73 dc) [11 sc & 9 dc]*

Row 8: (C2) BS, ch 1, 1 sc, [1 dc, 3 sc, 2 dc, 3 sc, 1 dc, 3 sc, 2 dc, 3 sc, 1 dc, 1 sc] 8 times, ch 1, BS. *(107 sc & 56 dc) [13 sc & 7 dc]*

Row 9: (C1) BS, ch 1, 1 sc, [1 sc, 2 dc, (3 sc, 2 dc) 3 times, 2 sc] 8 times, ch 1, BS. *(99 sc & 64 dc) [12 sc & 8 dc]*

Row 10: (C2) BS, ch 1, 1 dc, [3 sc, 2 dc, 3 sc, 1 dc, 1 sc, 1 dc, 3 sc, 2 dc, 3 sc, 1 dc] 8 times, ch 1, BS. *(106 sc & 57 dc) [13 sc & 7 dc]*

Row 11: (C1) BS, ch 1, 1 sc, [2 dc, 3 sc, 2 dc, 2 sc, 1 dc, 2 sc, 2 dc, 3 sc, 2 dc, 1 sc] 8 times, ch 1, BS. *(91 sc & 72 dc) [11 sc & 9 dc]*

Row 12: (C2) BS, ch 1, 1 sc, [2 sc, 2 dc, (3 sc, 1 dc) 2 times, 3 sc, 2 dc, 3 sc] 8 times, ch 1, BS. *(115 sc & 48 dc) [14 sc & 6 dc]*

Row 13: (C1) BS, ch 1, 1 dc, [1 dc, 3 sc, 2 dc, 2 sc, 1 dc, 1 sc, 1 dc, 2 sc, 2 dc, 3 sc, 2 dc] 8 times, ch 1, BS. *(90 sc & 73 dc) [11 sc & 9 dc]*

Row 14: (C2) BS, ch 1, 1 sc, [1 sc, 2 dc, 3 sc, (1 dc, 2 sc) 2 times, 1 dc, 3 sc, 2 dc, 2 sc] 8 times, ch 1, BS. *(107 sc & 56 dc) [13 sc & 7 dc]*

Row 15: (C1) BS, ch 1, 1 sc, [1 dc, 2 sc, 2 dc, 2 sc, 1 dc, 3 sc, 1 dc, 2 sc, 2 dc, 2 sc, 1 dc, 1 sc] 8 times, ch 1, BS. *(99 sc & 64 dc) [12 sc & 8 dc]*

Row 16: (C2) BS, ch 1, 1 dc, [5 sc, 1 dc, (3 sc, 1 dc) 2 times, 5 sc, 1 dc] 8 times, ch 1, BS. *(130 sc & 33 dc) [16 sc & 4 dc]*

Row 17: (C1) BS, ch 1, 1 sc, [1 dc, 2 sc, 2 dc, 2 sc, 1 dc, 3 sc, 1 dc, 2 sc, 2 dc, 2 sc, 1 dc, 1 sc] 8 times, ch 1, BS. *(99 sc & 64 dc) [12 sc & 8 dc]*

Row 18: (C2) BS, ch 1, 1 sc, [1 sc, 2 dc, 3 sc, 1 dc, (2 sc, 1 dc) 2 times, 3 sc, 2 dc, 2 sc] 8 times, ch 1, BS. *(107 sc & 56 dc) [13 sc & 7 dc]*

Row 19: (C1) BS, ch 1, 1 dc, [1 dc, 3 sc, 2 dc, 2 sc, 1 dc, 1 sc, 1 dc, 2 sc, 2 dc, 3 sc, 2 dc] 8 times, ch 1, BS. *(90 sc & 73 dc) [11 sc & 9 dc]*

Row 20: (C2) BS, ch 1, 1 sc, [2 sc, 2 dc, (3 sc, 1 dc) 2 times, 3 sc, 2 dc, 3 sc] 8 times, ch 1, BS. *(115 sc & 48 dc) [14 sc & 6 dc]*

Row 21: (C1) BS, ch 1, 1 sc, [2 dc, 3 sc, 2 dc, 2 sc, 1 dc, 2 sc, 2 dc, 3 sc, 2 dc, 1 sc] 8 times, ch 1, BS. *(91 sc & 72 dc) [11 sc & 9 dc]*

Row 22: (C2) BS, ch 1, 1 dc, [3 sc, 2 dc, 3 sc, 1 dc, 1 sc, 1 dc, 3 sc, 2 dc, 3 sc, 1 dc] 8 times, ch 1, BS. *(106 sc & 57 dc) [13 sc & 7 dc]*

Row 23: (C1) BS, ch 1, 1 sc, [1 sc, (2 dc, 3 sc) 3 times, 2 dc, 2 sc] 8 times, ch 1, BS. *(99 sc & 64 dc) [12 sc & 8 dc]*

Row 24: (C2) BS, ch 1, 1 sc, [1 dc, (3 sc, 2 dc, 3 sc, 1 dc) 2 times, 1 sc] 8 times, ch 1, BS. *(107 sc & 56 dc) [13 sc & 7 dc]*

Row 25: (C1) BS, ch 1, 1 dc, [2 sc, 2 dc, 3 sc, 2 dc, 1 sc, 2 dc, 3 sc, 2 dc, 2 sc, 1 dc] 8 times, ch 1, BS. *(90 sc & 73 dc) [11 sc & 9 dc]*

Row 26: (C2) BS, ch 1, 1 sc, [1 sc, 1 dc, 3 sc, 2 dc, 5 sc, 2 dc, 3 sc, 1 dc, 2 sc] 8 times, ch 1, BS. *(115 sc & 48 dc) [14 sc & 6 dc]*

Row 27: (C1) BS, ch 1, 1 sc, [1 dc, 2 sc, 2 dc, 4 sc, 1 dc, 4 sc, 2 dc, 2 sc, 1 dc, 1 sc] 8 times, ch 1, BS. *(107 sc & 56 dc) [13 sc & 7 dc]*

Row 28: (C2) BS, ch 1, 1 dc, [2 sc, 1 dc, 4 sc, 2 dc, 1 sc, 2 dc, 4 sc, 1 dc, 2 sc, 1 dc] 8 times, ch 1, BS. *(106 sc & 57 dc) [13 sc & 7 dc]*

Row 29: (C1) BS, ch 1, 1 sc, [1 sc, 1 dc, (2 sc, 3 dc, 2 sc, 1 dc) 2 times, 2 sc] 8 times, ch 1, BS. *(91 sc & 72 dc) [11 sc & 9 dc]*

Rows 30-225: Repeat Rows 2-29 *(28 rows)* seven times more.

BORDER

Follow instructions for Making the Border.

1. Secure the Yarn Tails.

2. Special Round: With right side facing, join C2 with standing sl st in first st on Foundation Row/Row 1; sl st around, working ch 2 in corners; join with sl st to first ch-2 sp. Cut yarn.
(163 sl sts across top and bottom edges, 225 sl sts across right and left edges & 4 corner ch-2 sps)

3. Back Layer:

Rnd 1: With wrong side facing, join C2 with standing dc in any corner ch-2 sp on bottom edge; (dc, ch 2, 2 dc) in same sp; dc in each st around *(taking care not to skip the sts before and after ch-2 corner sps)*, working (2 dc, ch 2, 2 dc) in each corner ch-2 sp; join with sl st to first *(standing)* dc. Do NOT cut yarn.
(167 dc across short sides, 229 dc across long sides & 4 corner ch-2 sps)

Rnd 2: (C2) Ch 3 *(counts as first dc)*, dc in next st, (2 dc, ch 2, 2 dc) in next corner ch-2 sp, dc in each st around, working (2 dc, ch 2, 2 dc) in each corner ch-2 sp; join with sl st to first dc (*3rd ch of beg ch-3*). Cut yarn. *(171 dc across short sides, 233 dc across long sides & 4 corner ch-2 sps)*

4. Front Layer:

Rnd 1: With right side facing, join C1 with standing sc in any corner ch-2 sp *(before dc-sts)*, ch 2, sc in same sp *(after the dc-sts)*, working in BLO of sl sts, sc in each st around, working (sc, ch 2, sc) in each corner; join with sl st to first sc. Cut yarn. *(165 sc across short sides, 227 sc across long sides & 4 corner ch-2 sps)*

Rnd 2 : Join C2 with standing sc in any corner ch-2 sp, ch 2, sc in same sp, working in BLO *(except corners)*, sc in each st around, working (sc, ch 2, sc) in each corner ch-2 sp; join with sl st to first sc. Do NOT cut yarn.

(167 sc across short sides, 229 sc across long sides & 4 corner ch-2 sps)

Rnds 3-4: (C2) Ch 1, sc in BLO of same st as joining, working in BLO *(except corners)*, sc in each st around, working (sc, ch 2, sc) in each corner ch-2 sp; join with sl st to first sc.

At the end of Round 4, cut yarn.

There are 171 sc across short sides, 233 sc across long sides & 4 corner ch-2 sps. (Every round has an increase of 2 stitches on each side.)

5. Join Front & Back Layers

Notes:

a. *The entire round is worked through the BLO of both the Front Layer and the corresponding Back Layer stitches together.*

b. *Corners are worked through the corresponding ch-2 spaces on both layers.*

Joining Round: With right side facing, join C2 with standing sc in any corner ch-2 sp, 2 sc in same sp; working in BLO, sl st in each st around, working 3 sc in each corner ch-2 sp; join with sl st to first sc. Cut yarn and sew in all ends. *(171 sl sts across short sides, 233 sl sts across long sides & 4 corner 3-sc)*

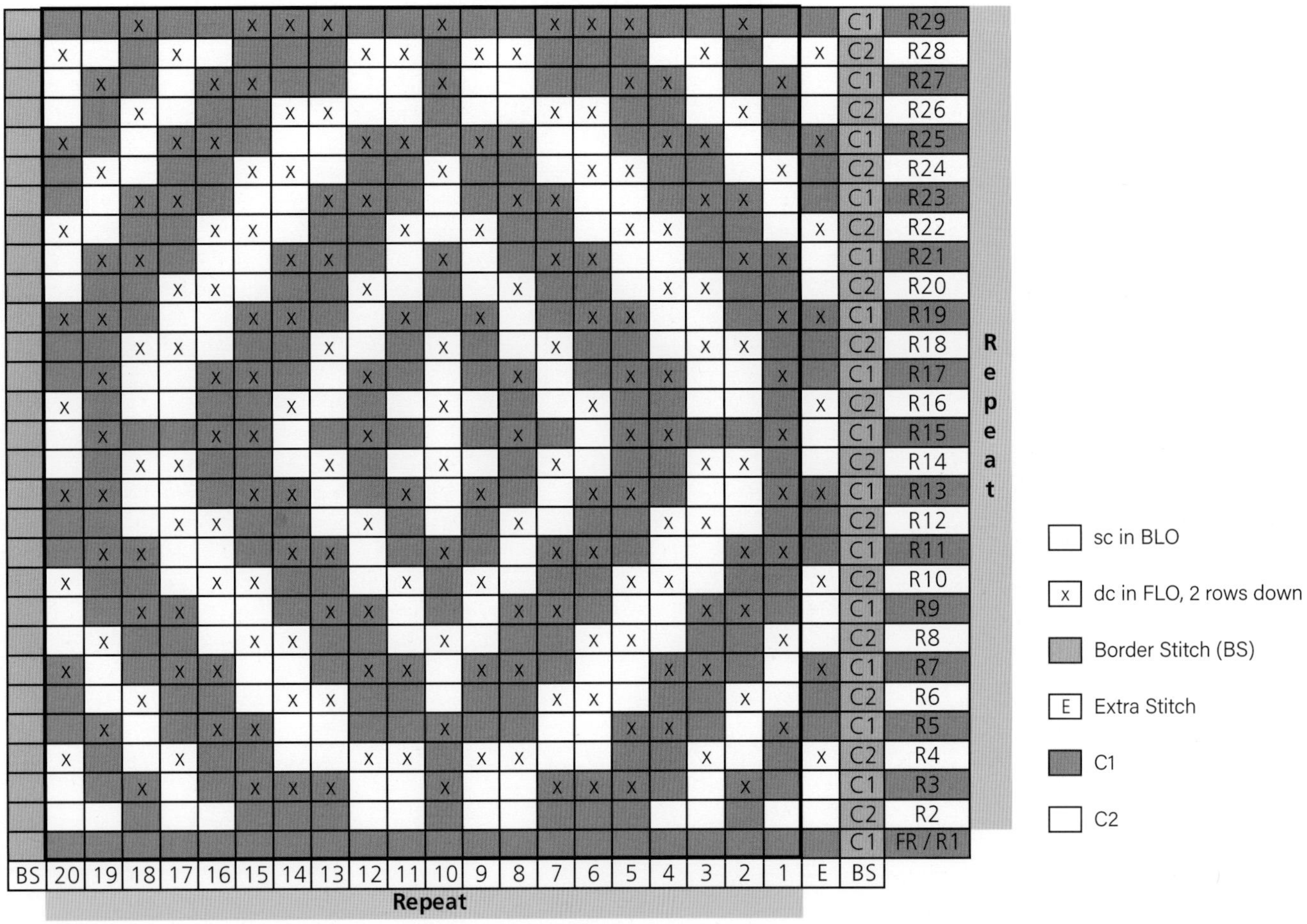

sc in BLO
dc in FLO, 2 rows down
Border Stitch (BS)
Extra Stitch
C1
C2
Repeat

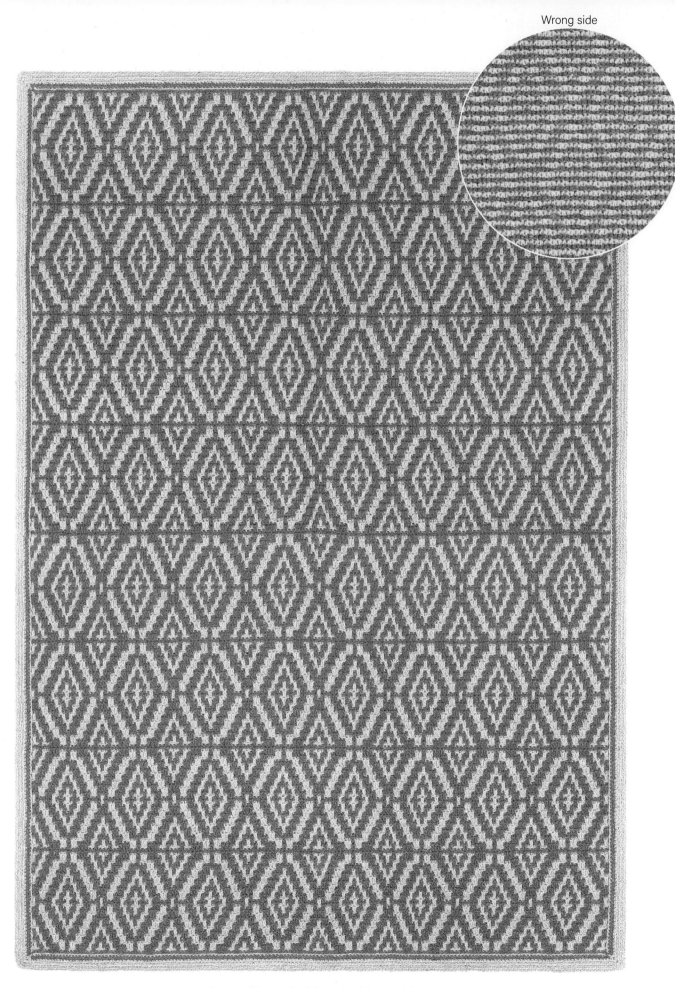

About 35″ (90 cm) wide and 49″ (125 cm) long

Winter
ELEMENTS

Materials

DK / Light Weight Yarn 🧶3 LIGHT

Queensland Walkabout (100% Wool)

1 ball - 1.76 oz (157 yards) / 50 g (144 m)

Color 1 (C1): Calypso (#24) – 7 balls

Color 2 (C2): Tundra (#23) – 8 balls

Color 3 (C3): Ecru (#01) – 8 balls

Size I-9 (5.5 mm) crochet hook (Blanket body and Special Round of the Border)

Size H-8 (5 mm) crochet hook (Front and Back Layers of the Border)

Scissors and Tapestry Needle

Finished Size & Gauge

Blanket: About 37" (95 cm) wide and 52" (132 cm) long.

Gauge: 17 stitches and 17 rows = 4" (10 cm) approximately.

Note: The finished size of the blanket might differ due to the gauge needed for the choice of yarn used. The overall size of the blanket can be customized by adding or removing pattern repeats, which will affect the amount of yarn required.

Multiple (Stitch Pattern Repeat): 20 + 3

There are 20 stitches in each pattern repeat.

The additional 3 stitches are the 2 Border Stitches plus 1 Extra Stitch at the beginning of a row.

Pattern Notes

❶ The Blanket pictured has 7 stitch pattern repeats.

❷ Refer to General Pattern Notes.

❸ See section on Special Stitches, if needed.

Skill Level

Intermediate or Adventurous Beginner

BLANKET

Foundation Row / Row 1: *(Right Side)* (C1) Using larger hook, make 143 FSC. Cut yarn. Do not turn your work. Continue with row 2. *(143 sc)*

Or for Chain Foundation:

Foundation Row / Row 1: *(Right Side)* (C1) Using larger hook, ch 144, starting in 2nd ch from hook, sc in each ch across. Cut yarn, leaving a tail. Do not turn your work. Continue with Row 2. *(143 sc)*

Row 2: (C2) BS, ch 1, 141 sc, ch 1, BS. *(143 sc)*

MAIN PATTERN

Rows 3-11: *(9 Rows)* Work Rows 1-9 from Pattern 1.

Rows 12-28: *(17 Rows)* Work Rows 1-17 from Pattern 2.

Rows 29-37: *(9 Rows)* Work Rows 1-9 from Pattern 3.

Rows 38-50: *(13 Rows)* Work Rows 1-13 from Pattern 4.

Rows 51-59: *(9 Rows)* Work Rows 1-9 from Pattern 1.

Rows 60-76: *(17 Rows)* Work Rows 1-17 from Pattern 5.

Rows 77-85: *(9 Rows)* Work Rows 1-9 from Pattern 3.

Rows 86-108: *(23 Rows)* Work Rows 1-23 from Pattern 6.

Rows 109-117: *(9 Rows)* Work Rows 1-9 from Pattern 1.

Rows 118-134: *(17 Rows)* Work Rows 1-17 from Pattern 5.

Rows 135-143: *(9 Rows)* Work Rows 1-9 from Pattern 3.

Rows 144-156: *(13 Rows)* Work Rows 1-13 from Pattern 4.

Rows 157-165: *(9 Rows)* Work Rows 1-9 from Pattern 1.

Rows 166-182: *(17 Rows)* Work Rows 1-17 from Pattern 2.

Rows 183-191: *(9 Rows)* Work Rows 1-9 from Pattern 3.

Row 192: (C2) BS, ch 1, 141 sc, ch 1, BS. (143 sc)

Row 193: (C1) BS, ch 1, 141 sc, ch 1, BS. (143 sc)

Continue with Border.

PATTERN 1:

Row 1: (C3) BS, ch 1, 141 sc, ch 1, BS. *(143 sc)*

Row 2: (C1) BS, ch 1, 141 sc, ch 1, BS. *(143 sc)*

Row 3: (C2) BS, ch 1, 141 sc, ch 1, BS. *(143 sc)*

Row 4: (C1) BS, ch 1, 141 sc, ch 1, BS. *(143 sc)*

Row 5: (C2) BS, ch 1, 1 sc, [(1 dc, 1 sc) 10 times] 7 times, ch 1, BS. *(73 sc & 70 dc) [10 sc & 10 dc]*

Row 6: (C1) BS, ch 1, 1 dc, [(3 sc, 1 dc) 5 times] 7 times, ch 1, BS. *(107 sc & 36 dc) [15 sc & 5 dc]*

Row 7: (C2) BS, ch 1, 1 sc, [(1 sc, 1 dc, 2 sc) 5 times] 7 times, ch 1, BS. *(108 sc & 35 dc) [15 sc & 5 dc]*

Row 8: (C1) BS, ch 1, 1 dc, [(1 dc, 1 sc, 2 dc) 5 times] 7 times, ch 1, BS. *(37 sc & 106 dc) [5 sc & 15 dc]*

Row 9: (C3) BS, ch 1, 141 sc, ch 1, BS. *(143 sc)*

Continue with Main Pattern.

PATTERN 2:

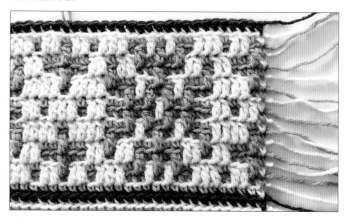

Row 1: (C2) BS, ch 1, 141 sc, ch 1, BS. *(143 sc)*

Row 2: (C3) BS, ch 1, 141 sc, ch 1, BS. *(143 sc)*

Row 3: (C1) BS, ch 1, 141 sc, ch 1, BS. *(143 sc)*

Row 4: (C3) BS, ch 1, 1 sc, [2 dc, 1 sc, 3 dc, 2 sc, 1 dc, 1 dc, 2 sc, 3 dc, 1 sc, 2 dc, 1 sc] 7 times, ch 1, BS. *(59 sc & 84 dc) [8 sc & 12 dc]*

Row 5: (C1) BS, ch 1, 1 dc, [7 sc, (1 dc, 1 sc) 2 times, 1 dc, 7 sc, 1 dc] 7 times, ch 1, BS. *(114 sc & 29 dc) [16 sc & 4 dc]*

Row 6: (C3) BS, ch 1, 1 sc, [2 sc, 2 dc, 1 sc, 2 dc, 5 sc, 2 dc, 1 sc, 2 dc, 3 sc] 7 times, ch 1, BS. *(87 sc & 56 dc) [12 sc & 8 dc]*

Row 7: (C1) BS, ch 1, 1 dc, [(4 sc, 1 dc) 4 times] 7 times, ch 1, BS. *(114 sc & 29 dc) [16 sc & 4 dc]*

Row 8: (C3) BS, ch 1, 1 sc, [4 dc, (3 sc, 1 dc) 2 times, 3 sc, 4 dc, 1 sc] 7 times, ch 1, BS. *(73 sc & 70 dc) [10 sc & 10 dc]*

Row 9: (C1) BS, ch 1, 1 sc, [6 sc, (1 dc, 1 sc) 3 times, 1 dc, 7 sc] 7 times, ch 1, BS. *(115 sc & 28 dc) [16 sc & 4 dc]*

Row 10: (C3) BS, ch 1, 1 dc, [1 dc, 1 sc, 2 dc, 5 sc, 1 dc, 5 sc, 2 dc, 1 sc, 2 dc] 7 times, ch 1, BS. *(86 sc & 57 dc) [12 sc & 8 dc]*

Row 11: (C1) BS, ch 1, 1 sc, [6 sc, (1 dc, 1 sc) 3 times, 1 dc, 7 sc] 7 times, ch 1, BS. *(115 sc & 28 dc) [16 sc & 4 dc]*

Row 12: (C3) BS, ch 1, 1 sc, [4 dc, (3 sc, 1 dc) 2 times, 3 sc, 4 dc, 1 sc] 7 times, ch 1, BS. *(73 sc & 70 dc) [10 sc & 10 dc]*

Row 13: (C1) BS, ch 1, 1 dc, [(4 sc, 1 dc) 4 times] 7 times, ch 1, BS. *(114 sc & 29 dc) [16 sc & 4 dc]*

Row 14: (C3) BS, ch 1, 1 sc, [2 sc, 2 dc, 1 sc, 2 dc, 5 sc, 2 dc, 1 sc, 2 dc, 3 sc] 7 times, ch 1, BS. *(87 sc & 56 dc) [12 sc & 8 dc]*

Row 15: (C1) BS, ch 1, 1 dc, [7 sc, (1 dc, 1 sc) 2 times, 1 dc, 7 sc, 1 dc] 7 times, ch 1, BS. *(114 sc & 29 dc) [16 sc & 4 dc]*

Row 16: (C3) BS, ch 1, 1 sc, [2 dc, 1 sc, 3 dc, 2 sc, 1 dc, 1 sc, 1 dc, 2 sc, 3 dc, 1 sc, 2 dc, 1 sc] 7 times, ch 1, BS. *(59 sc & 84 dc) [8 sc & 12 dc]*

Row 17: (C2) BS, ch 1, 141 sc, ch 1, BS. *(143 sc)*

Continue with Main Pattern.

Pattern 1

BS	20	19	18	17	16	15	14	13	12	11	10	9	8	7	6	5	4	3	2	1	E	BS	Color	Row
BS																						BS	C3	R9
BS	x	x		x	x	x		x	x	x		x	x	x		x	x	x		x	x	BS	C1	R8
BS			x			x				x				x				x					BS	C2	R7
BS	x				x				x				x				x					x	BS	C1	R6
BS		x		x		x		x		x		x		x		x		x		x			BS	C2	R5
BS																							BS	C1	R4
BS																							BS	C2	R3
BS																							BS	C1	R2
BS																							BS	C3	R1

Repeat

Legend: sc in BLO | **x** dc in FLO, 2 rows down | Border Stitch (BS) | E Extra Stitch | C1 | C2 | C3

Pattern 2

BS	20	19	18	17	16	15	14	13	12	11	10	9	8	7	6	5	4	3	2	1	E	BS	Color	Row
BS																							BS	C2	R17
BS		x	x		x	x	x			x		x			x	x	x		x	x			BS	C3	R16
BS		x							x		x		x									x	BS	C1	R15
BS					x	x		x	x					x	x		x	x					BS	C3	R14
BS		x					x						x									x	BS	C1	R13
BS		x	x	x	x					x				x			x	x	x	x			BS	C3	R12
BS							x		x		x		x										BS	C1	R11
BS		x	x		x	x						x					x	x		x	x	x	BS	C3	R10
BS							x		x		x		x										BS	C1	R9
BS		x	x	x	x					x				x			x	x	x	x			BS	C3	R8
BS		x					x						x									x	BS	C1	R7
BS					x	x		x	x					x	x		x	x					BS	C3	R6
BS		x							x		x		x									x	BS	C1	R5
BS		x	x		x	x	x			x		x			x	x	x		x	x			BS	C3	R4
BS																							BS	C1	R3
BS																							BS	C3	R2
BS																							BS	C2	R1

Repeat

Legend: sc in BLO | **x** dc in FLO, 2 rows down | Border Stitch (BS) | E Extra Stitch | C1 | C2 | C3

PATTERN 3

Row 1: (C3) BS, ch 1, 141 sc, ch 1, BS. *(143 sc)*

Row 2: (C1) BS, ch 1, 141 sc, ch 1, BS. *(143 sc)*

Row 3: (C2) BS, ch 1, 141 sc, ch 1, BS. *(143 sc)*

Row 4: (C1) BS, ch 1, 1 dc, [(1 dc, 1 sc, 2 dc) 5 times] 7 times, ch 1, BS. *(37 sc & 106 dc) [5 sc & 15 dc]*

Row 5: (C2) BS, ch 1, 1 sc, [(1 sc, 1 dc, 2 sc) 5 times] 7 times, ch 1, BS. *(108 sc & 35 dc) [15 sc & 5 dc]*

Row 6: (C1) BS, ch 1, 1 dc, [(3 sc, 1 dc) 5 times] 7 times, ch 1, BS. *(107 sc & 36 dc) [15 sc & 5 dc]*

Row 7: (C2) BS, ch 1, 1 sc, [(1 dc, 1 sc) 10 times] 7 times, ch 1, BS. *(73 sc & 70 dc) [10 sc & 10 dc]*

Row 8: (C1) BS, ch 1, 141 sc, ch 1, BS. *(143 sc)*

Row 9: (C3) BS, ch 1, 141 sc, ch 1, BS. *(143 sc)*

Continue with Main Pattern.

PATTERN 4

Row 1: (C2) BS, ch 1, 141 sc, ch 1, BS. *(143 sc)*

Row 2: (C3) BS, ch 1, 141 sc, ch 1, BS. *(143 sc)*

Row 3: (C2) BS, ch 1, 1 sc, [1 sc, (1 dc, 2 sc) 2 times, 1 dc, 3 sc, (1 dc, 2 sc) 3 times] 7 times, ch 1, BS. *(101 sc & 42 dc) [14 sc & 6 dc]*

Row 4: (C3) BS, ch 1, 1 dc, [3 sc, 1 dc, 1 sc, (1 dc, 3 sc) 2 times, 1 dc, 1 sc, 1 dc, 3 sc, 1 dc] 7 times, ch 1, BS. *(100 sc & 43 dc) [14 sc & 6 dc]*

Row 5: (C2) BS, ch 1, 1 sc, [2 sc, 1 dc, 3 sc, 1 dc, 5 sc, (1 dc, 3 sc) 2 times] 7 times, ch 1, BS. *(115 sc & 28 dc) [16 sc & 4 dc]*

Row 6: (C3) BS, ch 1, 1 sc, [(1 dc, 3 sc) 2 times, 1 dc, 1 sc, (1 dc, 3 sc) 2 times, 1 dc, 1 sc] 7 times, ch 1, BS. *(101 sc & 42 dc) [14 sc & 6 dc]*

Row 7: (C2) BS, ch 1, 1 sc, [3 sc, 1 dc, 1 sc, 1 dc, 7 sc, 1 dc, 1 sc, 1 dc, 4 sc] 7 times, ch 1, BS. *(115 sc & 28 dc) [16 sc & 4 dc]*

Row 8: (C3) BS, ch 1, 1 sc, [1 sc, 1 dc, 5 sc, 1 dc, 3 sc, 1 dc, 5 sc, 1 dc, 2 sc] 7 times, ch 1, BS. *(115 sc & 28 dc) [16 sc & 4 dc]*

Row 9: (C2) BS, ch 1, 1 sc, [4 sc, 1 dc, 9 sc, 1 dc, 5 sc] 7 times, ch 1, BS. *(129 sc & 14 dc) [18 sc & 2 dc]*

Row 10: (C3) BS, ch 1, 1 sc, [2 sc, 1 dc, 3 sc, 1 dc, 5 sc, (1 dc, 3 sc) 2 times] 7 times, ch 1, BS. *(115 sc & 28 dc) [16 sc & 4 dc]*

Row 11: (C2) BS, ch 1, 1 sc, [4 sc, 1 dc, 9 sc, 1 dc, 5 sc] 7 times, ch 1, BS. *(129 sc & 14 dc) [18 sc & 2 dc]*

Row 12: (C3) BS, ch 1, 1 sc, [3 sc, 1 dc, 1 sc, 1 dc, 7 sc, 1 dc, 1 sc, 1 dc, 4 sc] 7 times, ch 1, BS. *(115 sc & 28 dc) [16 sc & 4 dc]*

Row 13: (C2) BS, ch 1, 141 sc, ch 1, BS. *(143 sc)*

Continue with Main Pattern.

Pattern 3

BS	20	19	18	17	16	15	14	13	12	11	10	9	8	7	6	5	4	3	2	1	E	BS		
																							C3	R9
																							C1	R8
		x		x		x		x		x		x		x		x		x		x			C2	R7
	x				x				x				x				x				x		C1	R6
			x				x				x				x				x				C2	R5
	x	x			x	x	x		x	x	x			x	x	x			x		x		C1	R4
																							C2	R3
																							C1	R2
																							C3	R1

Repeat

☐ sc in BLO   **x** dcin FLO, 2 rows down   ▨ Border Stitch (BS)   E Extra Stitch   ▨ C1   ▨ C2   ☐ C3

Pattern 4

BS	20	19	18	17	16	15	14	13	12	11	10	9	8	7	6	5	4	3	2	1	E	BS		
																							C2	R13
					x		x							x		x							C3	R12
						x										x							C2	R11
				x				x					x				x						C3	R10
						x										x							C2	R9
			x						x			x							x				C3	R8
					x		x							x		x							C2	R7
		x				x				x	x				x				x				C3	R6
			x					x					x				x						C2	R5
	x				x		x				x			x		x					x		C3	R4
			x			x			x			x				x			x				C2	R3
																							C3	R2
																							C2	R1

Repeat

☐ sc in BLO   **x** dcin FLO, 2 rows down   ▨ Border Stitch (BS)   E Extra Stitch   ▨ C1   ▨ C2   ☐ C3

79

PATTERN 5

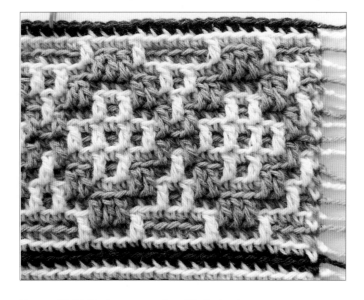

Row 1: (C2) BS, ch 1, 141 sc, ch 1, BS. *(143 sc)*

Row 2: (C3) BS, ch 1, 141 sc, ch 1, BS. *(143 sc)*

Row 3: (C1) BS, ch 1, 141 sc, ch 1, BS. *(143 sc)*

Row 4: (C3) BS, ch 1, 1 sc, [(2 sc, 1 dc, 3 sc, 1 dc, 5 sc, (1 dc, 3 sc) 2 times] 7 times, ch 1, BS. *(115 sc & 28 dc) [16 sc & 4 dc]*

Row 5: (C1) BS, ch 1, 1 sc, [3 sc, 3 dc, 7 sc, 3 dc, 4 sc] 7 times, ch 1, BS. *(101 sc & 42 dc) [14 sc & 6 dc]*

Row 6: (C3) BS, ch 1, 1 sc, [(1 dc, 7 sc, 1 dc, 1 sc) 2 times] 7 times, ch 1, BS. *(115 sc & 28 dc) [16 sc & 4 dc]*

Row 7: (C1) BS, ch 1, 1 sc, [1 sc, (2 dc, 3 sc) 3 times, 2 dc, 2 sc] 7 times, ch 1, BS. *(87 sc & 56 dc) [12 sc & 8 dc]*

Row 8: (C3) BS, ch 1, 1 dc, [(3 sc, 1 dc, 1 sc, 1 dc, 3 sc, 1 dc) 2 times] 7 times, ch 1, BS. *(100 sc & 43 dc) [14 sc & 6 dc]*

Row 9: (C1) BS, ch 1, 1 sc, [(1 dc, 7 sc, 1 dc, 1 sc) 2 times] 7 times, ch 1, BS. *(115 sc & 28 dc) [16 sc & 4 dc]*

Row 10: (C3) BS, ch 1, 1 sc, [1 sc, (1 dc, 1 sc) 4 times, 2 sc, (1 dc, 1 sc) 4 times, 1 sc] 7 times, ch 1, BS. *(87 sc & 56 dc) [12 sc & 8 dc]*

Row 11: (C1) BS, ch 1, 1 sc, [(1 dc, 7 sc, 1 dc, 1 sc) 2 times] 7 times, ch 1, BS. *(115 sc & 28 dc) [16 sc & 4 dc]*

Row 12: (C3) BS, ch 1, 1 dc, [(3 sc, 1 dc, 1 sc, 1 dc, 3 sc, 1 dc) 2 times] 7 times, ch 1, BS. *(100 sc & 43 dc) [14 sc & 6 dc]*

Row 13: (C1) BS, ch 1, 1 sc, [1 sc, (2 dc, 3 sc) 3 times, 2 dc, 2 sc] 7 times, ch 1, BS. *(87 sc & 56 dc) [12 sc & 8 dc]*

Row 14: (C3) BS, ch 1, 1 sc, [(1 dc, 7 sc, 1 dc, 1 sc) 2 times] 7 times, ch 1, BS. *(115 sc & 28 dc) [16 sc & 4 dc]*

Row 15: (C1) BS, ch 1, 1 sc, [3 sc, 3 dc, 7 sc, 3 dc, 4 sc] 7 times, ch 1, BS. *(101 sc & 42 dc) [14 sc & 6 dc]*

Row 16: (C3) BS, ch 1, 1 sc, [2 sc, 1 dc, 3 sc, 1 dc, 5 sc, (1 dc, 3 sc) 2 times] 7 times, ch 1, BS. *(115 sc & 28 dc) [16 sc & 4 dc]*

Row 17: (C2) BS, ch 1, 141 sc, ch 1, BS. *(143 sc)*

Continue with Main Pattern.

PATTERN 6

Row 1: (C2) BS, ch 1, 141 sc, ch 1, BS. *(143 sc)*

Row 2: (C3) BS, ch 1, 141 sc, ch 1, BS. *(143 sc)*

Row 3: (C2) BS, ch 1, 141 sc, ch 1, BS. *(143 sc)*

Row 4: (C3) BS, ch 1, 1 sc, [(3 dc, 3 sc, 3 dc, 1 sc) 2 times] 7 times, ch 1, BS. *(59 sc & 84 dc) [8 sc & 12 dc]*

Row 5: (C2) BS, ch 1, 1 dc, [(4 sc, 1 dc) 4 times] 7 times, ch 1, BS. *(114 sc & 29 dc) [16 sc & 4 dc]*

Row 6: (C3) BS, ch 1, 1 sc, [(1 sc, 3 dc) 2 times, 3 sc, 3 dc, 1 sc, 3 dc, 2 sc] 7 times, ch 1, BS. *(59 sc & 84 dc) [8 sc & 12 dc]*

Row 7: (C2) BS, ch 1, 1 sc, [1 dc, 7 sc, 3 dc, 7 sc, 1 dc, 1 sc] 7 times, ch 1, BS. *(108 sc & 35 dc) [15 sc & 5 dc]*

Row 8: (C3) BS, ch 1, 1 dc, [3 sc, 3 dc, 7 sc, 3 dc, 3 sc, 1 dc] 7 times, ch 1, BS. *(93 sc & 50 dc [13 sc & 7 dc]*

Row 9: (C2) BS, ch 1, 1 sc, [1 sc, 2 dc, 3 sc, 3 dc, 1 sc, 3 dc, 3 sc, 2 dc, 2 sc] 7 times, ch 1, BS. *(73 sc & 70 dc) [10 sc & 10 dc]*

Row 10: (C3) BS, ch 1, 1 dc, [3 sc, 3 dc, 7 sc, 3 dc, 3 sc, 1 dc] 7 times, ch 1, BS. *(93 sc & 50 dc) [13 sc & 7 dc]*

Row 11: (C2) BS, ch 1, 1 sc, [1 dc, 7 sc, 3 dc, 7 sc, 1 dc, 1 sc] 7 times, ch 1, BS. *(108 sc & 35 dc) [15 sc & 5 dc]*

Row 12: (C3) BS, ch 1, 1 sc, [(1 sc, 3 dc) 2 times, 3 sc, 3 dc, 1 sc, 3 dc, 2 sc] 7 times, ch 1, BS. *(59 sc & 84 dc) [8 sc & 12 dc]*

Row 13: (C2) BS, ch 1, 1 dc, [(4 sc, 1 dc) 4 times] 7 times, ch 1, BS. *(114 sc & 29 dc) [16 sc & 4 dc]*

Row 14: (C3) BS, ch 1, 1 sc, [(3 dc, 3 sc, 3 dc, 1 sc) 2 times] 7 times, ch 1, BS. *(59 sc & 84 dc) [8 sc & 12 dc]*

Row 15: (C2) BS, ch 1, 1 sc, [3 sc, 1 dc, 1 sc, 1 dc, 7 sc, 1 dc, 1 sc, 1 dc, 4 sc] 7 times, ch 1, BS. *(115 sc & 28 dc) [16 sc & 4 dc]*

Row 16: (C3) BS, ch 1, 1 dc, [1 dc, 7 sc, 3 dc, 7 sc, 2 dc] 7 times, ch 1, BS. *(100 sc & 43 dc) [14 sc & 6 dc]*

Row 17: (C2) BS, ch 1, 1 sc, [(1 sc, 1 dc) 4 times, 3 sc, (1 dc, 1 sc)

Row 18: (C3) BS, ch 1, 1 dc, [1 dc, 7 sc, 3 dc, 7 sc, 2 dc] 7 times, ch 1, BS. *(100 sc & 43 dc) [14 sc & 6 dc]*

Row 19: (C2) BS, ch 1, 1 sc, [3 sc, 1 dc, 1 sc, 1 dc, 7 sc, 1 dc, 1 sc, 1 dc, 4 sc] 7 times, ch 1, BS. *(115 sc & 28 dc) [16 sc & 4 dc]*

Row 20: (C3) BS, ch 1, 1 sc, [(3 dc, 3 sc, 3 dc, 1 sc) 2 times] 7 times, ch 1, BS. *(59 sc & 84 dc) [8 sc & 12 dc]*

Row 21: (C2) BS, ch 1, 1 dc, [(4 sc, 1 dc) 4 times] 7 times, ch 1, BS. *(114 sc & 29 dc) [16 sc & 4 dc]*

Row 22: (C3) BS, ch 1, 1 sc, [(1 sc, 3 dc) 2 times, 3 sc, 3 dc, 1 sc, 3 dc, 2 sc] 7 times, ch 1, BS. *(59 sc & 84 dc) [8 sc & 12 dc]*

Row 23: (C2) BS, ch 1, 141 sc, ch 1, BS. *(143 sc)*

Continue with Main Pattern.

Pattern 5

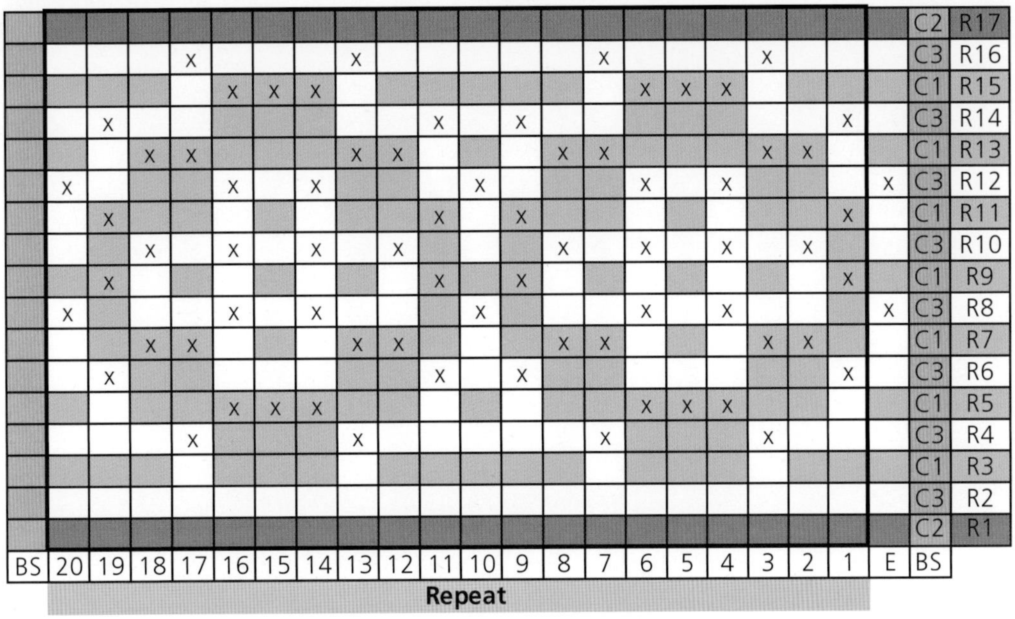

BS	20	19	18	17	16	15	14	13	12	11	10	9	8	7	6	5	4	3	2	1	E	BS	

Row colors (top to bottom): C2 R17, C3 R16, C1 R15, C3 R14, C1 R13, C3 R12, C1 R11, C3 R10, C1 R9, C3 R8, C1 R7, C3 R6, C1 R5, C3 R4, C1 R3, C3 R2, C2 R1

Repeat

Legend: ☐ sc in BLO | **x** dc in FLO, 2 rows down | ▨ Border Stitch (BS) | E Extra Stitch | ☐ C1 | ▪ C2 | ☐ C3

Pattern 6

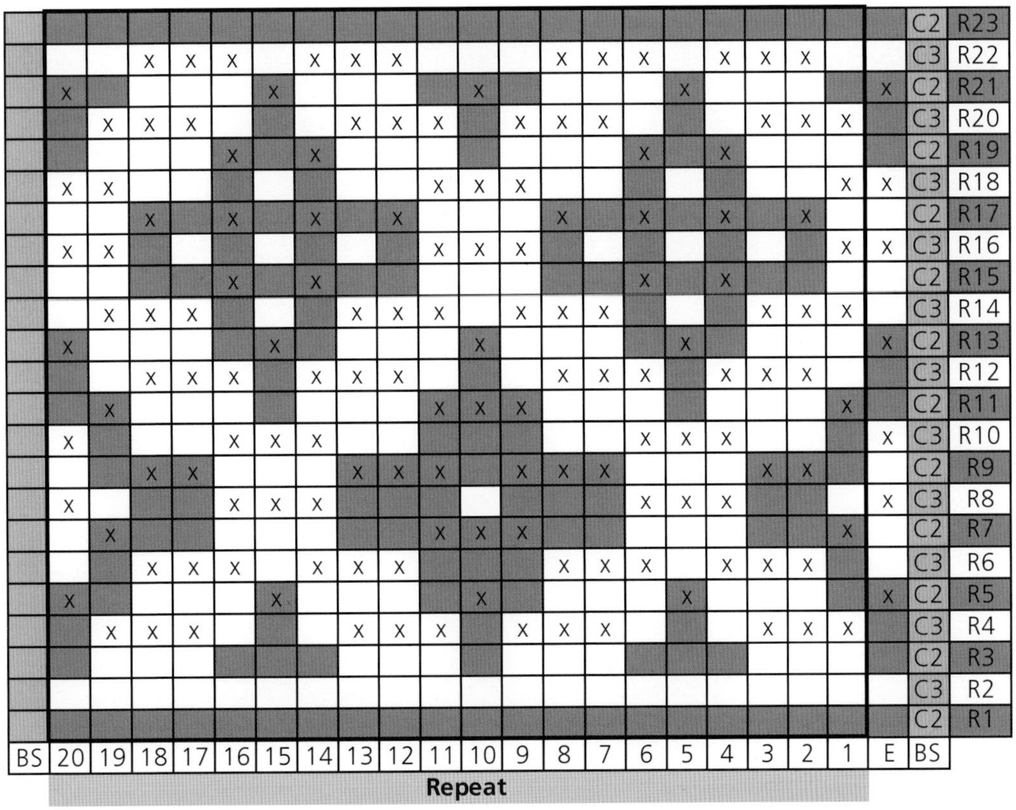

BS	20	19	18	17	16	15	14	13	12	11	10	9	8	7	6	5	4	3	2	1	E	BS	

Row colors (top to bottom): C2 R23, C3 R22, C2 R21, C3 R20, C2 R19, C3 R18, C2 R17, C3 R16, C2 R15, C3 R14, C2 R13, C3 R12, C2 R11, C3 R10, C2 R9, C3 R8, C2 R7, C3 R6, C2 R5, C3 R4, C2 R3, C3 R2, C2 R1

Repeat

Legend: ☐ sc in BLO | **x** dc in FLO, 2 rows down | ▨ Border Stitch (BS) | E Extra Stitch | ☐ C1 | ▪ C2 | ☐ C3

81

BORDER

Follow instructions for Making the Border.

1. Secure the Yarn Tails.

2. Special Round: With right side facing, using larger hook, join C2 with standing sl st in first st on Foundation Row/Row 1; sl st around, working ch 2 in corners; join with sl st to first ch-2 sp. Cut yarn. *(143 sl sts across top and bottom edges, 193 sl sts across right and left edges & 4 corner ch-2 sps)*

3. Back Layer:

Note: On the short sides only, two additional stitches need to be added: [dc in each of next 70 sts, 2 dc in next st] 2 times, then continue across to corner.

Rnd 1: With wrong side facing, using smaller hook, join C2 with standing dc in any corner ch-2 sp on bottom edge; (dc, ch 2, 2 dc) in same sp; dc in each st around *(taking care not to skip the sts before and after ch-2 corner sps)*, working (2 dc, ch 2, 2 dc) in each corner ch-2 sp *(remembering to add the extra stitches on the short sides)*; join with sl st to first *(standing)* dc. Do NOT cut yarn. *(149 dc across short sides, 197 dc across long sides & 4 corner ch-2 sps)*

Rnd 2: (C2) Ch 3 *(counts as first dc)*, dc in next st, (2 dc, ch 2, 2 dc) in next corner ch-2 sp, dc in each st around, working (2 dc, ch 2, 2 dc) in each corner ch-2 sp; join with sl st to first dc (*3rd* ch of beg ch-3). Do NOT cut yarn. *(153 dc across short sides, 201 dc across long sides & 4 corner ch-2 sps)*

Rnd 3: (C2) Ch 1, sc in same st as joining, sc in each st around, working (sc, ch 2, sc) in each corner ch-2 sp; join with sl st to first sc. Cut yarn. *(155 dc across short sides, 203 dc across long sides & 4 corner ch-2 sps)*

4. Front Layer:

Note:

On the short sides only, two additional stitches need to be added: [sc in each of next 70 sts, 2 sc in next st] 2 times, then continue across to corner.

Rnd 1: With right side facing, using smaller hook, join C2 with standing sc in any corner ch-2 sp *(before dc-sts)*, ch 2, sc in same sp *(after the dc-sts)*, working in BLO of sl sts, sc in each st around *(remembering to add the extra stitches on the short sides)*, working (sc, ch 2, sc) in each corner; join with sl st to first sc. Cut yarn. *(147 sc across short sides, 195 sc across long sides & 4 corner ch-2 sps)*

Rnd 2: (C1) Join C1 with standing sc in any corner ch-2 sp, ch 2, sc in same sp, working in BLO *(except corners)*, sc in each st around, working (sc, ch 2, sc) in each corner ch-2 sp; join with sl st to first sc. Cut yarn. *(149 sc across short sides, 197 sc across long sides & 4 corner ch-2 sps)*

Notes:

1. For Rnds 3 to 5, single crochet stitches are worked in back loop only (except corners) and double crochet stitches are worked in the front loop only of the corresponding stitch 2 rounds below.

2. The stitch count on every round increases by 2 stitches on each side.)

Rnd 3: (C2) Join C2 with standing sc in any corner ch-2 sp before a long side, ch 2, sc in same sp, working (sc, ch 2, sc) in each corner, work across the Sides as follows:

Long Sides:

1 sc, 4 dc, [3 sc, 1 dc] 47 times, 3 dc, 1 sc

Short Sides:

1 sc, 4 dc, [3 sc, 1 dc] 35 times, 3 dc, 1 sc

At the end of the round; join with sl st to first sc. Cut yarn. *(109 sc & 42 dc across short sides (151 sts), 145 sc & 54 dc across long sides (199 sts) & 4 corner ch-2 sps)*

Rnd 4: (C1) Join C1 with standing sc in any corner ch-2 sp before a long side, ch 2, sc in same sp, working (sc, ch 2, sc) in each corner, work across the Sides as follows:

Long Sides:

6 sc, [1 dc, 1 sc] 94 times, 5 sc

Short Sides:

6 sc, [1 dc, 1 sc] 70 times, 5 sc

At the end of the round; join with sl st to first sc. Cut yarn. *(83 sc & 70 dc across short sides (153 sts), 107 sc & 94 dc across long sides (201 sts) & 4 corner ch-2 sps)*

Rnd 5: (C2) Join C2 with standing sc in any corner ch-2 sp before a long side, ch 2, sc in same sp, working (sc, ch 2, sc) in each corner, work across the Sides as follows:

Long Sides:

1 sc, 6 dc, [3 sc, 1 dc] 47 times, 5 dc, 1 sc

Short Sides:

1 sc, 6 dc, [3 sc, 1 dc] 35 times, 5 dc, 1 sc

At the end of the round; join with sl st to first sc. Cut yarn. *(109 sc & 46 dc across short sides (155 sts), 145 sc & 58 dc across long sides (203 sts) & 4 corner ch-2 sps)*

5. Join Front & Back Layers

Notes:

a. The entire round is worked through the BLO of both the Front Layer and the corresponding Back Layer stitches together.

b. Corners are worked through the corresponding ch-2 spaces on both layers.

Joining Round: With right side facing, using smaller hook, join C2 with standing sc in any corner ch-2 sp, 2 sc in same sp; working in BLO, sl st in each st around, working 3 sc in each corner ch-2 sp; join with sl st to first sc. Cut yarn and sew in all ends.
(155 sl sts across short sides, 203 sl sts across long sides & 4 corner 3-sc)

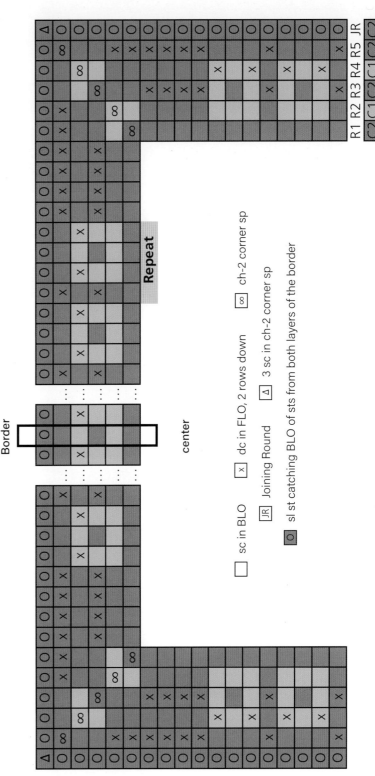

Legend:

- ☐ sc in BLO
- ☒ dc in FLO, 2 rows down
- JR Joining Round
- 8 ch-2 corner sp
- △ 3 sc in ch-2 corner sp
- ▢ sl st catching BLO of sts from both layers of the border

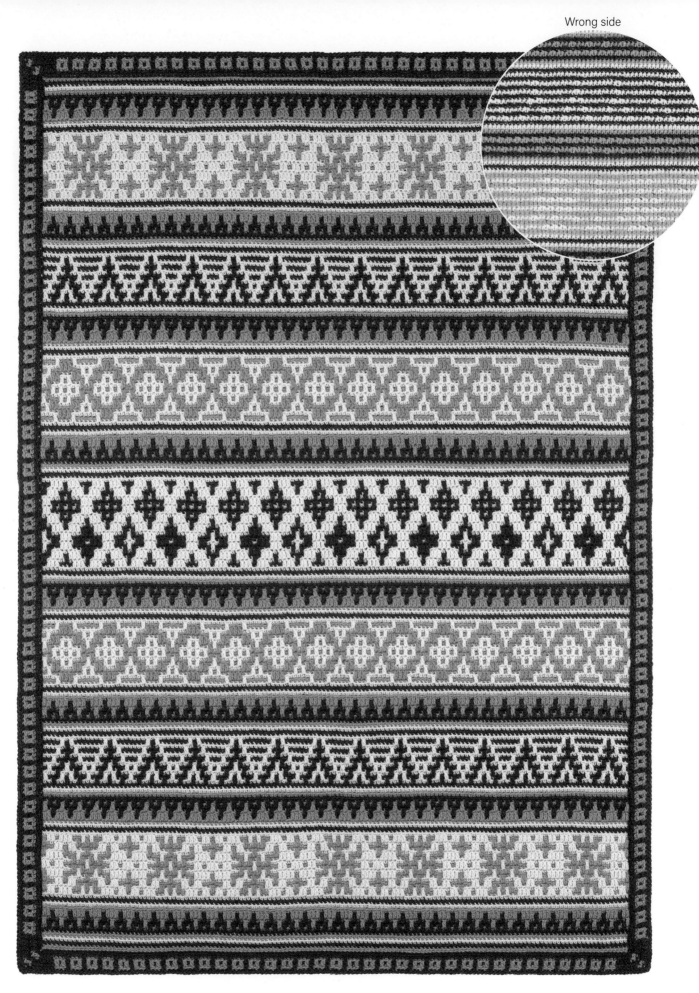

Wrong side

About 37" (95 cm) wide and 52" (132 cm) long.

in my GARDEN

Materials

Worsted / Medium Weight Yarn

Juniper Moon Farm Moonshine (40% Alpaca, 40% Wool, 20% Organic Silk)

1 ball – 3.52 oz (197 yards)/ 100 g (180 m)

> **Color 1 (C1):** Moonbeam (#02) – 6 balls
>
> **Color 2 (C2):** Charcoal (#16) – 6 balls
>
> **Color 3 (C3):** Mustard (#56) – 2 balls

Size I-9 (5.5 mm) crochet hook (Blanket Body and Special Round of the Border)

Size H-8 (5 mm) crochet hook (Front and Back Layers of the Border)

4″ (10 cm) wide piece of Card (for Tassels)

Scissors and Tapestry Needle

Finished Size & Gauge

Blanket: About 35″ (90 cm) wide and 43″ (110 cm) long

Gauge: 16 stitches and 16 rows = 4″ (10 cm) approximately.

Note: The finished size of the blanket might differ due to the gauge needed for the choice of yarn used. The overall size of the blanket can be customized by adding or removing pattern repeats, which will affect the amount of yarn required.

Multiple (Stitch Pattern Repeat): 18 + 5

There are 18 stitches in each pattern repeat.

The additional 5 stitches are the 2 Border Stitches plus 2 Extra Stitches at the beginning of a row and 1 Extra Stitch at the end of the row.

Pattern Notes

1️⃣ The Blanket pictured has 7 stitch pattern repeats.

2️⃣ Refer to General Pattern Notes.

3️⃣ See section on Special Stitches, if needed.

Skill Level

Intermediate or Adventurous Beginner

BLANKET

Foundation Row / Row 1: *(Right Side)* (C1) Using larger hook, make 131 FSC. Cut yarn. Do not turn your work. Continue with Row 2. (131 sc)

Or for Chain Foundation:

Foundation Row / Row 1: *(Right Side)* (C1) Using larger hook, ch 132, starting in 2nd ch from hook, sc in each ch across. Cut yarn, leaving a tail. Do not turn your work. Continue with Row 2. (131 sc)

Row 2: (C2) BS, ch 1, 129 sc, ch 1, BS. *(131 sc)*

Row 3: (C1) BS, ch 1, 1 dc, 1 sc, [6 dc, (1 sc, 1 dc) 2 times, 1 sc, 6 dc, 1 sc] 7 times, 1 dc, ch 1, BS.
(31 sc & 100 dc) [4 sc & 14 dc]

Row 4: (C2) BS, ch 1, 1 sc, 1 dc, [17 sc, 1 dc] 7 times, 1 sc, ch 1, BS.
(123 sc & 8 dc) [17 sc & 1 dc]

Row 5: (C1) BS, ch 1, 1 dc, 1 sc, [2 sc, 4 dc, (1 sc, 1 dc) 2 times, 1 sc, 4 dc, 3 sc] 7 times, 1 dc, ch 1, BS.
(59 sc & 72 dc) [8 sc & 10 dc]

Row 6: (C2) BS, ch 1, 1 sc, 1 dc, [1 sc, 1 dc, 4 sc, (1 dc, 1 sc) 2 times, 1 dc, 4 sc, 1 dc, 1 sc, 1 dc] 7 times, 1 dc, ch 1, BS.
(88 sc & 43 dc) [12 sc & 6 dc]

Repeat Begins:

Row 7: (C1) BS, ch 1, 1 dc, 1 sc, [1 dc, 3 sc, 2 dc, 5 sc, 2 dc, 3 sc, 1 dc, 1 sc] 7 times, 1 dc, ch 1, BS.
(87 sc & 44 dc) [12 sc & 6 dc]

Row 8: (C2) BS, ch 1, 1 sc, 1 dc, [3 sc, (1 dc, 4 sc) 2 times, 1 dc, 3 sc, 1 dc] 7 times, 1 sc, ch 1, BS.
(102 sc & 29 dc) [14 sc & 4 dc]

Row 9: (C1) BS, ch 1, 1 dc, 1 sc, [2 sc, 1 dc, 3 sc, 2 dc, 1 sc, 2 dc, 3 sc, 1 dc, 3 sc] 7 times, 1 dc, ch 1, BS.
(87 sc & 44 dc) [12 sc & 6 dc]

Row 10: (C2) BS, ch 1, 1 sc, 1 dc, [1 sc, 1 dc, 3 sc, (1 dc, 2 sc) 2 times, 1 dc, 3 sc, 1 dc, 1 sc, 1 dc] 7 times, 1 sc, ch 1, BS.
(88 sc & 43 dc) [12 sc & 6 dc]

Row 11: (C1) BS, ch 1, 1 dc, 1 sc, [1 dc, 3 sc, 1 dc, 2 sc, 1 dc, 1 sc, 1 dc, 2 sc, 1 dc, 3 sc, 1 dc, 1 sc] 7 times, 1 dc, ch 1, BS.
(87 sc & 44 dc) [12 sc & 6 dc]

Row 12: (C2) BS, ch 1, 1 sc, 1 dc, [(1 sc, 1 dc) 2 times, 2 sc, (1 dc, 1 sc) 2 times, 1 dc, 2 sc, (1 dc, 1 sc) 2 times, 1 dc] 7 times, 1 sc, ch 1, BS. *(74 sc & 57 dc) [10 sc & 8 dc]*

Row 13: (C1) BS, ch 1, 1 dc, 1 sc, [1 dc, 3 sc, 2 dc, (1 sc, 1 dc) 2 times, 1 sc, 2 dc, 3 sc, 1 dc, 1 sc] 7 times, 1 dc, ch 1, BS.
(73 sc & 58 dc) [10 sc & 8 dc]

Row 14: (C2) BS, ch 1, 1 sc, 1 dc, [6 sc, (1 dc, 1 sc) 2 times, 1 dc, 6 sc, 1 dc] 7 times, 1 sc, ch 1, BS.
(102 sc & 29 dc) [14 sc & 4 dc]

Row 15: (C1) BS, ch 1, 1 dc, 1 sc, [2 sc, 3 dc, 2 sc, 1 dc, 1 sc, 1 dc, 2 sc, 3 dc, 3 sc] 7 times, 1 dc, ch 1, BS.
(73 sc & 58 dc) [10 sc & 8 dc]

Row 16: (C2) BS, ch 1, 1 sc, 1 dc, [1 sc, 1 dc, 3 sc, (1 dc, 2 sc) 2 times, 1 dc, 3 sc, 1 dc, 1 sc, 1 dc] 7 times, 1 sc, ch 1, BS.
(88 sc & 43 dc) [12 sc & 6 dc]

Row 17: (C1) BS, ch 1, 1 dc, 1 sc, [1 dc, 1 sc, 1 dc, 3 sc, 2 dc, 1 sc, 2 dc, 3 sc, (1 dc, 1 sc) 2 times] 7 times, 1 dc, ch 1, BS.
[73 sc & 58 dc] [10 sc & 8 dc]

Row 18: (C2) BS, ch 1, 1 sc, 1 dc, [3 sc, (1 dc, 4 sc) 2 times, 1 dc, 3 sc, 1 dc] 7 times, 1 sc, ch 1, BS.
(102 sc & 29 dc) [14 sc & 4 dc]

Row 19: (C1) BS, ch 1, 1 dc, 1 sc, [1 dc, 3 sc, 2 dc, 5 sc, 2 dc, 3 sc, 1 dc, 1 sc] 7 times, 1 dc, ch 1, BS.
(87 sc & 44 dc) [12 sc & 6 dc]

Row 20: (C2) BS, ch 1, 1 sc, 1 dc, [1 sc, 1 dc, 4 sc, (1 dc, 1 sc) 2 times, 1 dc, 4 sc, 1 dc, 1 sc, 1 dc] 7 times, 1 sc, ch 1, BS.
(88 sc & 43 dc) [12 sc & 6 dc]

Row 21: (C1) BS, ch 1, 1 dc, 1 sc, [2 sc, 2 dc, 3 sc, 1 dc, 1 sc, 1 dc, 3 sc, 2 dc, 3 sc] 7 times, 1 dc, ch 1, BS.
(87 sc & 44 dc) [12 sc & 6 dc]

Row 22: (C2) BS, ch 1, 1 sc, 1 dc, [4 sc, (1 dc, 3 sc) 2 times, 1 dc, 4 sc, 1 dc] 7 times, 1 sc, ch 1, BS.
(102 sc & 29 dc) [14 sc & 4 dc]

Row 23: (C1) BS, ch 1, 1 dc, 1 sc, [2 dc, 3 sc, 1 dc, 5 sc, 1 dc, 3 sc, 2 dc, 1 sc] 7 times, 1 dc, ch 1, BS.
(87 sc & 44 dc) [12 sc & 6 dc]

Row 24: (C2) BS, ch 1, 1 sc, 1 dc, [2 sc, 1 dc, 3 sc, (1 dc, 1 sc) 2 times, 1 dc, 3 sc, 1 dc, 2 sc, 1 dc] 7 times, 1 sc, ch 1, BS.
(88 sc & 43 dc) [12 sc & 6 dc]

Row 25: (C1) BS, ch 1, 1 dc, 1 sc, [1 dc, 2 sc, 1 dc, 3 sc, 1 dc, 1 sc, 1 dc, 3 sc, 1 dc, 2 sc, 1 dc, 1 sc] 7 times, 1 dc, ch 1, BS.
(87 sc & 44 dc) [12 sc & 6 dc]

Row 26: (C2) BS, ch 1, 1 sc, 1 dc, [1 sc, 1 dc, 2 sc, (1 dc, 1 sc) 4 times, 1 dc, 2 sc, 1 dc, 1 sc, 1 dc] 7 times, 1 sc, ch 1, BS.
(74 sc & 57 dc) [10 sc & 8 dc]

Row 27: (C1) BS, ch 1, 1 dc, 1 sc, [1 dc, 1 sc, 2 dc, 3 sc, 1 dc, 1 sc, 1 dc, 3 sc, 2 dc, 1 sc, 1 dc, 1 sc] 7 times, 1 dc, ch 1, BS.
(73 sc & 58 dc) [10 sc & 8 dc]

Row 28: (C2) BS, ch 1, 1 sc, 1 dc, [1 sc, (1 dc, 6 sc) 2 times, 1 dc, 1 sc, 1 dc] 7 times, 1 sc, ch 1, BS.
(102 sc & 29 dc) [14 sc & 4 dc]

Row 29: (C1) BS, ch 1, 1 dc, 1 sc, [1 dc, 2 sc, 3 dc, 5 sc, 3 dc, 2 sc, 1 dc, 1 sc] 7 times, 1 dc, ch 1, BS.
(73 sc & 58 dc) [10 sc & 8 dc]

Row 30: (C2) BS, ch 1, 1 sc, 1 dc, [2 sc, 1 dc, 3 sc, (1 dc, 1 sc) 2 times, 1 dc, 3 sc, 1 dc, 2 sc, 1 dc] 7 times, 1 sc, ch 1, BS.
(88 sc & 43 dc) [12 sc & 6 dc]

Row 31: (C1) BS, ch 1, 1 dc, 1 sc, [2 dc, 3 sc, (1 dc, 1 sc) 3 times, 1 dc, 3 sc, 2 dc, 1 sc] 7 times, 1 dc, ch 1, BS.
(73 sc & 58 dc) [10 sc & 8 dc]

Row 32: (C2) BS, ch 1, 1 sc, 1 dc, [4 sc, (1 dc, 3 sc) 2 times, 1 dc, 4 sc, 1 dc] 7 times, 1 sc, ch 1, BS.
(102 sc & 29 dc) [14 sc & 4 dc]

Row 33: (C1) BS, ch 1, 1 dc, 1 sc, [2 sc, 2 dc, 3 sc, 1 dc, 1 sc, 1 dc, 3 sc, 2 dc, 3 sc] 7 times, 1 dc, ch 1, BS.
(87 sc & 44 dc) [12 sc & 6 dc]

Row 34: (C2) BS, ch 1, 1 sc, 1 dc, [1 sc, 1 dc, 4 sc, (1 dc, 1 sc) 2 times, 1 dc, 4 sc, 1 dc, 1 sc, 1 dc] 7 times, 1 sc, ch 1, BS.
(88 sc & 43 dc) [12 sc & 6 dc]

Rows 35-146: Repeat Rows 7-34 *(28 rows)* four times more.

Rows 147-160: Repeat Rows 7-20 *(14 rows)*.

Row 161: Repeat Row 5.

Row 162: Repeat Row 4.

Row 163: Repeat Row 3.

BORDER

Follow instructions for Making the Border.

1. Secure the Yarn Tails.

2. Special Round: With right side facing, using larger hook, join C3 with standing sl st in first st on Foundation Row/Row 1; sl st around, working ch 2 in corners; join with sl st to first ch-2 sp. Cut yarn. *(131 sl sts across top and bottom edges, 163 sl sts across right and left edges & 4 corner ch-2 sps)*

3. Back Layer:

Rnd 1: With wrong side facing, using smaller hook, join C3 with standing dc in any corner ch-2 sp on bottom edge; (dc, ch 2, 2 dc) in same sp; dc in each st around *(taking care not to skip the sts before and after ch-2 corner sps)*, working (2 dc, ch 2, 2 dc) in each corner ch-2 sp; join with sl st to first *(standing)* dc. Do NOT cut yarn. *(135 dc across short sides, 167 dc across long sides & 4 corner ch-2 sps)*

Rnd 2: (C3) Ch 3 *(counts as first dc)*, dc in next st, (2 dc, ch 2, 2 dc) in next corner ch-2 sp, dc in each st around, working (2 dc, ch 2, 2 dc) in each corner ch-2 sp; join with sl st to first dc *(3rd ch of beg ch-3)*. Cut yarn. *(139 dc across short sides, 171 dc across long sides & 4 corner ch-2 sps)*

4. Front Layer:

Rnd 1: With right side facing, using smaller hook, join C3 with standing sc in any corner ch-2 sp *(before dc-sts)*, ch 2, sc in same sp *(after the dc-sts)*, working in BLO of sl sts, sc in each st around, working (sc, ch 2, sc) in each corner; join with sl st to first sc. Do NOT cut yarn. *(133 sc across short sides, 165 sc across long sides & 4 corner ch-2 sps)*

Rnds 2-3: (C3) Ch 1, sc in BLO of same st as joining, working in BLO *(except corners)*, sc in each st around, working (sc, ch 2, sc) in each corner ch-2 sp; join with sl st to first sc.

At the end of Round 3, cut yarn.

There are 137 sc across short sides, 169 sc across long sides & 4 corner ch-2 sps. (Every round has an increase of 2 stitches on each side.)

Rnd 4: Join C2 with standing sc in any corner ch-2 sp, ch 2, sc in same sp, working in BLO *(except corners)*, sc in each st around, working (sc, ch 2, sc) in each corner ch-2 sp; join with sl st to first sc. Cut yarn.
(139 sc across short sides, 171 sc across long sides & 4 corner ch-2 sps)

5. Join Front & Back Layers

Notes:

a. *The entire round is worked through the BLO of both the Front Layer and the corresponding Back Layer stitches together.*

b. *Corners are worked through the corresponding ch-2 spaces on both layers.*

Joining Round: With right side facing, using smaller hook, join C2 with standing sc in any corner ch-2 sp, 2 sc in same sp; working in BLO, sl st in each st around, working 3 sc in each corner ch-2 sp; join with sl st to first sc. Cut yarn and sew in all ends. *(139 sl sts across short sides, 171 sl sts across long sides & 4 corner 3-sc)*

FINAL TOUCH

A tassel is attached to each corner of the Blanket.

Tassel (Make 4) *Refer to Making A Tassel.*

Preparation:

1. Cut a piece of card 4" (10 cm) wide

2. Long lengths *(6 strands):*
Cut two 30" (75 cm) strands of each color yarn (2 x Color 1, 2 x Color 2 & 2 x Color 3).

3. Short Lengths *(2 strands):*
Cut two 20" (50 cm) strands of Color 2.

Method:
Follow steps 1 to 8 of Making a Tassel Method, wrapping the yarn three times around the card in step 1.

Repeat for each Tassel.

Repeat
Repeat

sc in BLO
x dc in FLO, 2 rows down
Border Stitch (BS)
E Extra Stitch
C1
C2

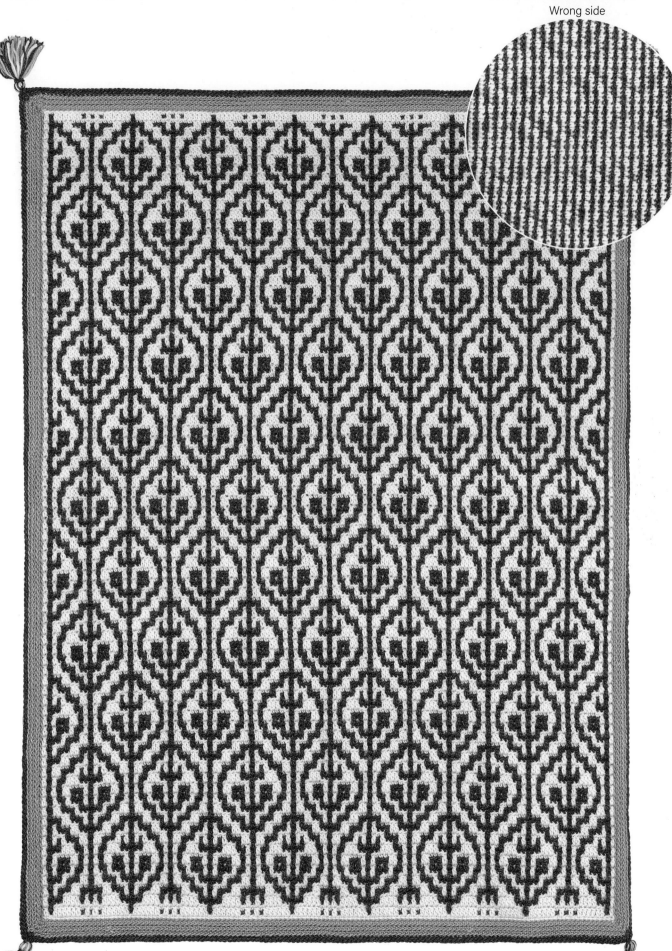

About 35" (90 cm) wide and 43" (110 cm) long